Your Life is Worth Living

Your Life is Worth Living

INSPIRATIONAL DEVOTIONS
FOR WOMEN

by
BETTY CARLSON

ZONDERVAN PUBLISHING HOUSE
A DIVISION OF THE ZONDERVAN CORPORATION
GRAND RAPIDS, MICHIGAN

Formerly published as
LIFE IS FOR LIVING
Copyright 1962 by
Zondervan Publishing House
Grand Rapids, Michigan

First printing ..... April, 1962
Second printing .... May, 1962
Third printing 1963
Fourth printing 1965
Fifth printing 1966
Sixth printing 1968
Seventh printing 1969
Eighth printing 1970
Ninth printing 1971
Tenth printing 1972

This book is dedicated to Frances Pitts
and Eugenia Price, and to my mother and
theirs. They will know why.

INTRODUCTION

As the curtain falls on *Vanity Fair*, Thackeray walks downstage center and says, "Ah! *Vanitas Vanitatum!* Which of us is happy in this world? Which of us has his desire? or, having it, is satisfied? — Come, children, let us shut up the box and the puppets, for our play is played out."

Thackeray's story is finished, but yours isn't nor mine. Some of us yet have many years ahead of us, others only a question of months or days. None of us knows. But whatever the time, be it long or short, I for one am truly interested in making the most of the time I still have; and I have an idea you are too, or you would not be bothering with this book.

Life is for living, not for sighing, moaning, and groaning about how difficult our lot is, how complicated everything is today, how evil the times; nor is life for regretting. We all have our share of tragic mistakes, wrong choices, foolish decisions.

I spent six years of my life studying to be a specialist in the field of recreation. There was a time when I could name every bone and muscle in the body. Also, I knew all the rules and by-laws for every major and minor sport known to frolicsome man. For my thesis I wrote a monumental paper on the organization of intramural programs in small colleges. I still have a foot locker bulging with notes and books on the principles of physical education, folk games, and posture control.

And it took three days of teaching to know this was not my calling. In fact, as I pondered the situation, I realized that the only reason I had majored in physical education was that I liked to play tennis and swim. I still do.

In the interim I have occasionally thought what a colossal waste of time it was to spend six years training for a specific field and never put that knowledge to use. However, recently I have become increasingly aware of the truth that nothing is wasted in God's world. Nothing. In fact, some of our most valuable lessons are learned negatively.

So it took me six years and three days to learn that I am not a teacher, and another seventeen curious, meandering years to learn a lot of other things I am not; but how else could God teach me that life isn't what it seems? that there is much, much more to life than meets the natural eye, that only a few men live up to the marvelous potential God has placed in them, but many more could; that once we think we have arrived, we surely haven't; that there are as many wet, gloomy days in a year as sunny; that often we pray, but seldom do we wait; we ask, but we really don't expect to receive; we knock, but off we run before the way is made open.

This book will teach you nothing new. I am in agreement with Solomon, "There is nothing new under the sun." I can only serve you as "a remembrancer." Daily you and I who want to live more fully need to remind ourselves that what we need is not necessarily greater faith, but faith in a greater God. We need to be more hopeful about God and His strength and less occupied with our smallness and frailty. In the midst of our ordinary, everyday duties we need to learn to live expectantly. As F. B. Meyer once said, "No one can know the day or hour when God passes by, seeking for chosen vessels and goodly pearls. When least expecting it, we are being scrutinized, in daily commonplaces, to see if we shall be faithful in more momentous issues. Let us be always on the alert, our loins girt, our lamps burning, our nets mended and cleansed."

The thought occurred to me one morning, Why couldn't someone work out some spiritual exercises? If there is one thing I learned in my six years of physical education training, it is to respect systematic exercising. Even the most stubborn, stout bodies bend a little when subjected to calisthenics. Why couldn't one's spiritual health be improved if one deliberately worked at it? It surely would not hurt to try to bend lower and reach higher spiritually, because it is in this realm of our living that we are going to find the real answers to how to make the most of the time we still have. I, for one, am willing to give this a try. Won't you join me? Thank you.

BETTY CARLSON

January, 1962

Your Life is Worth Living

PART 1

Cheerfully

1

MANY ARE OUR WOES

Small Talk: As I slipped and sloshed my way to work on the third day of spring, my thoughts were as gloomy as the weather. So this is the golden age of the machine! Give me the tin from the old days when women baked bread and children and men shoveled snow.

Today it is not only unpleasant but perilous to take a winter walk. Having gingerly moved my brittle frame over ice-packed, rutted sidewalks for the past five months, I better appreciate the expression, "He died with his boots on!"

To get the most out of living, it helps to be simple-minded and cheerful. The two go together. In *The Tempest,* Shakespeare puts these words in the mouth of Gonzalo:

"Beseech you, sir, be merry. . . . Our occasion of woe is common."

We Northerners share the common woe of snow. Most of the people I know hate snow. Simply groan when they see it. O, children and dogs and a few like myself don't, but speaking in general terms, snow is not popular anymore.

It is sort of foolish, I think. If I am forced to spend several months with someone, it is easier on my nervous system if I attempt to find *something* attractive about that person. It is much the same with snow.

I dare say there is not a person reading this page who is going to outlive snow. So "be merry, our occasion of woe is common." If you can't beat them, join them. Work on your attitude.

Try smiling the next time you reach for the shovel. Think what it is doing for your waistline, your lungs, your pallid cheeks.

Most of us are in better shape than Stanley Cherry of Saginaw, Michigan. This 73-year-old gentleman finds that his wheel chair slows him only slightly when it comes to shoveling snow. He improvised a shovel out of a broom stick and dust pan and takes pride in keeping his walks clear.

I haven't noticed that many people in my town take pride in keeping their walks clear. The only place in my neighborhood where you can step out freely is in front of the four taverns and two funeral parlors.

I don't imagine that I would have written this soliloquy on snow if on this third day of spring my feet hadn't gone out from under me on an unshoveled walk in my town. As I sat upon the ice and snow, I made a solemn pledge with myself to write about this topic, providing, of course, every bone in my body wasn't broken and I wasn't disabled for life.

Being the contemplative sort, or in the words of Jean Kerr, "a low-metabolism type," I am just now getting around to this snow essay on a lovely spring day when I couldn't care less if people never lifted a shovel as long as they live.

All I long to do today is walk.

Walk and simply delight in the wonder of living.

These are the happiest days, after the snow and before the crab grass. As I walk, I am going to think about attitude — my attitude. O God, help me to be merry for the sake of others, to live simply because therein is depth, and to be brimming with cheer, because Thou art with me now and forever — summer, winter, autumn and this beautiful spring; and remind me, come next fall (or spring), that I like snow.

Spiritual Exercise: Concentrate on one of these stumblers in your life — snow, grass, dishes, correcting papers, calling on sick friends, washing the car, writing to relatives, cleaning your room. Pray for a noticeable change in attitude, then go do it. (If you are like me, you will have several changes of attitude to pray about, and certain irritants that keep popping back; so this exercise may be used over and over with profit not only to you, but your family and friends, and your community.)

2

GOD'S PROBLEM

Small Talk: When some of us were in the yard the other night with heads tipped back straining to get a glimpse of Echo, different ones kept supplying bits of information about this man-made satellite — how fast it was going, how far away it was, etc. One friend, as she lowered her head and started to work the kinks out of her neck, said,

"I don't think I'd believe it, but there it is. I can see it for myself."

We're all this way, to a certain extent; particularly about truth. I am somewhat this way about a statement Paul made. My reserve and caution tell me to do what some Biblical interpreters do — look for the "spiritual" message; but my childlike trust in Christ and that side of my nature that enjoys adventure overrule and cause me to accept these words just as they are written.

Listen! Have you ever heard anything as intriguing? At a certain point in historical time (Paul doesn't give us the date) the Lord Himself is going to descend from heaven. And as the Bible says, "With the shout of an archangel, and with the blast of the trumpet of God."

And that's not all. Paul says that those who have already died will rise first. Then we (you and all the other believers) shall simultaneously be caught up in the clouds (with the resurrected dead — there will be many of those dear ones who have gone before us), and together we shall meet the Lord in the air. And Paul finishes this fantastic announcement by telling us that from that momentous moment we shall be with the Lord, on and on, through the eternity of the eternities.

I find these words marvelously comforting and encouraging in the face of the deep, deep troubles we are in here on earth.

From time to time I have pondered why we find these words of Paul hard "to swallow." Because we do. In the past nine years I have visited many different churches, and I have never heard a sermon on this subject. Is it because the thought of actually meeting the Lord in the air seems too hilarious, too unconventional, too exhilarating to be a facet in a respectable religion?

Religion, it would appear, is supposed to be staid and proper, even a little dull; but if any man will examine it for himself, this is not at all the case in authentic Christianity.

Christianity has many extraordinary elements. Indeed it is exhilarating and hilarious to think of taking off into space someday without the necessity of standing in line to buy a ticket on a rocket. My nephew and I were talking about this the other day, and he was a little concerned how it would work. But we decided that this isn't our problem. It is God's. Our part is to believe and, as Paul suggests, to encourage ourselves with this hope. It helps to take the sting out of the gigantic question mark Russia has dangling over our heads, "What happens if there is a nuclear war?"

Louis Cheskin, a motivational research expert, has recently been probing the subconscious worries of thousands of Americans. He has found that the worry over a nuclear war overwhelms all other concerns of the average American. In Mr. Cheskin's words, "People can't define their anxieties. They even say that everything is fine. But subconsciously there is great disturbance, especially fear of a nuclear war."

Faith is the only destroyer of fear. Real faith. We must not only read the Word of God, but believe it; not take plain words and claim they don't really mean what they say.

It is quite possible the world is not going to end today or tomorrow. It is a curious fact of history that nearly every generation has scanned the future with foreboding. Erasmus spoke of the sixteenth century as "the excrement of the ages." I bet there will be some eye-opening comments made about the twentieth century.

There have been mournful, bleeding epitaphs scratched on each page of history; but man is still here, still going on, still muddling through. The real victors have always been those who go cheerfully on, knowing whether we live or die, it is gain.

My mother usually ends her letters to me with a Bible verse that had meaning for her that day, plus these words, "Keep busy, keep happy."

Spiritual Exercise: In either prone or sitting position, ask yourself what you think these words of Paul mean: "For the Lord himself shall descend from heaven with a shout, with the voice of the archangel, and with the trump of God: and the dead in Christ shall rise first: Then we which are alive and remain shall be caught up together with them in the clouds, to meet the Lord in the air: and so shall we ever be with the Lord."

3

AIM FOR CHEERFULNESS

Small Talk: "If there is anything I have learned from living that has helped me to keep my equilibrium," a handsome woman in her seventies said recently, "it is to accept the fact that frustration and problems are as much a part of living as getting up every morning and going to bed every night.

"And the second thing," she added, "if at all possible, is to aim for cheerfulness. You won't always hit it, but you'll never regret having tried to see the brighter side."

She explained further that when she was a young woman and involved in one of her first bewildering problems, she thought, *Now if I can just get through this.* A suggestion of a smile came into her eyes, "I honestly thought that I'd never again experience that sinking feeling of total inadequacy." She shook her head. "Within two years I was involved in a situation that made the earlier problem seem like a box lunch social in comparison. I have learned that each age has its peculiar problems, and there is no time when we may sit back and say, 'I have slain all the dragons on this road.'"

Obviously this friend has found a dragon-eradicator, because she is still cheerfully going about her business. There is one other reason why her life has been meaningful, and her niece expressed it this way, "My aunt is a religious person."

Hers is the quiet, steady sort. She seldom talks about it. I doubt that she has ever prayed in a group or been a leader in the church; but the sure, real spark is there.

She simply lives her faith.

She quietly believes these grand, lilting words Christ left with His disciples shortly before He was arrested and crucified, "Be of good cheer! I have overcome the world."

Spiritual Exercise: Ask God to remove whatever trial seems more than you can endure; and then if, after a reasonable time, He doesn't, thank Him for giving you the inner resources to bear so great a burden.

As Marcus Antoninus said: "Remember, on every occasion which leads thee to vexation to apply this principle: that this is not a misfortune, but that to bear it nobly is good fortune."

4

GIVE ME MUSIC

Small Talk: I believe it is Piglet, possibly Pooh, who remarks that there is nothing that cheers like a balloon. In the lovely world of the enchanted forest Milne created for us in his *Winnie-the-Pooh* stories, this is true. But in my down-to-earth, real world of right now, I find there is nothing that cheers like music.

I am a little suspicious of the person who announces, "I care for only classical music." It is a little like saying that you enjoy only "educated" people. Frankly, when it comes to music and people, I find my interest is spread over a wide range. I, too, have an appreciation for classical music. You don't play an oboe for fifteen years without learning to love symphonies, concertos, and woodwind quintets. But along with my enthusiasm for "long hair" music, there are times when I find there is nothing that cheers quite like a march or a waltz or a Swedish polka. There is a vast amount of music in the semi-classical range and popular field that I find stimulating also, and I don't see how anyone can resist a lovely folk tune or cowboy music when done tastefully.

And so when I was invited to a junior high school band concert recently, I went willingly. While waiting for the concert to begin, we were noticing different people coming into the auditorium. My sister-in-law remarked, "I wonder why Bill Johnson is here?"

When she quickly added, "Oh sure, he's here because his grandson plays the flute in the eighth grade band. . . ." I had one of those flash illuminations. It had never occurred to me until that minute that one of the reasons all the different concerts I had played in as a youngster were so well attended — I had lots of relatives.

If I had even vaguely suspected that the better half of every concert audience I had played for had been coerced into coming, it would have dampened my dedication. I was a serious artist in my junior and senior high days, and I always blew my best for the music lovers of Rockford.

I attended this band concert both as a music lover and relative, and happily I am sure that that is a rather common combination. It was a fine concert, and I would have felt cheated had I not been there. What a great advantage it is to have music in one's life. I always feel extra hopeful about a young person when I know he loves music.

There was one disappointment that night. Not one of the three bands played a Sousa march. I am strictly of the opinion that there is nothing that cheers quite like a Sousa march.

No, there is nothing that cheers like music. I can remember one night in Holland. I was on a bicycle trip and I had gone to Rotterdam to visit a certain museum I had read about. I had thought I could find lodging in the city, but it never really got through to me how thorough the Nazis had been in their destruction of that city until I cycled through the heart of the city and hardly found a building standing, and this was a few years after the war. It depressed me so, I didn't have the heart to ask if the museum I was seeking also was destroyed. I simply rode away. Some hours later I found myself in a strange, small village. It was dark, and I was tired. I had one of those rare moments when I felt alone and afraid. All of a sudden I heard some music ahead. Never did a Salvation Army band sound so good. There they stood on a busy corner in front of a noisy inn playing "What a Friend We Have in Jesus." I'm sure the artistic quality of their playing was not much better than a group I hear on Clark Street here in Chicago once in awhile, but to my ears, it was celestial music.

I was unable to converse with the players — I knew no Dutch and they knew no English — but I was able to communicate my gratitude to them for the cheerful concert. They seemed to understand I needed lodging for the evening, and they steered me to a quiet, respectable inn on another street.

Nothing cheers like music. Nothing cheers quite as much as the grand psalms and hymns that have burst the bonds of loneliness, multiplied difficulties and sadness. Often they have risen out of dreadful hours that leave scars on the hearts of men, and they meet us in our despairing moments. The good music of the church also meets us in our happy moments. I, for one, would be lost without good music.

Spiritual Exercise: Turn to your favorite hymn. Read the words, really pay attention to what they say. Then sing all verses softly.

5

TRAVEL NONCHALANCE

Small Talk: One afternoon I was taking an afternoon siesta. "When in Rome, do as the Romans do." Only this was Florence, a few hundred miles north. Sightseeing is strenuous. You have to relax in between museums and cathedrals or you'd never make

it back home. Shortly after I closed my eyes, I was vaguely conscious that my bed was swaying, but I was at that stage of museum-
and-cathedral fatigue when the brain isn't functioning too clearly;
so it didn't really register with me how *odd* this was.

Then, too, one gets so used to having unusual things happen
on a trip that one develops what I call "travel nonchalance." Like
when I was in Hawaii once, I was served pickled octopus. You
would have thought I had been brought up on the rubbery stuff,
I was so poised when I ate it. This is "travel nonchalance." It takes
years to develop. Some never do.

Back to Italy: when this slight rocking motion happened
again while we were having dinner on the roof garden of our hotel
two hours later, and the lady at the next table gave her husband a
wide-eyed look and gasped, "Did you feel that?" I realized this
must be an earthquake. What else makes beds sway and chan-
deliers swing?

Our waiter had considerable "travel nonchalance." He continued serving our dinner as if nothing had happened. I tried to
learn from him if earthquakes are routine in Florence. He didn't
understand. Every time I said "earthquake," he sprinkled more
cheese on my spaghetti.

We didn't find out until the next week, when we were back
in Switzerland and someone remembered to buy a newspaper,
that, yes, Florence had had an earthquake that day. It was of such
severity just outside the city that several graves had split open and
tombstones had tumbled, but fortunately no one was killed.

I have often wished that I were more successful in holding
on to this spirit of "travel nonchalance" in my daily living. I have
about the same percentage of minor harassments, interruptions,
and small blows that you have. Like this morning my car wouldn't
start, and that walk to the nearest restaurant in zero weather
seemed pretty snappy, and the man in the filling station didn't
seem too interested in pushing my car; now why can't I smile about
these inconveniences? If I were on a trip in a foreign country,
these minor things would only cause me to shrug my shoulders,
"So we have another day in Baghdad. Fine, let's make the most
of it."

I think I'm closer to the answer now. I'm not looking for

things to run smoothly when I travel, but when I'm home, I do; and it truly is not only unreasonable, but unrealistic. "In the world you shall have tribulation . . ." minor and major, whether at home or abroad. And it does gladden the tiresomely impatient heart to remember those cheerful words, "I have overcome the world."

Spiritual Exercise: So my car didn't start this morning. Thank You, Lord, for the five or six hundred times it has started in the past year. (You may make up your own prayer that fits your vexation.) Help us all, dear God, not to waste energy on "little things." May we be discerning and save our impatience for the big things we ought to be excited about.

PART 2

Hopefully

6

ALL THE WAY HOME

Small Talk: We were riding in the country on a summer day when we passed the cemetery. My uncle commented, "That land has been in our family for a long time." I turned back to look again at the small family graveyard with the inviting shade trees and green grass. I know that was their land, but I had almost forgotten the little cemetery. No one said anything, and then my aunt murmured softly in Swedish, "Där skall vi ligga en dag."

I don't know much Swedish, but I understood that, "there shall we lie someday," and her remark never left me. Life went on for several months, and then last Saturday on a cold winter day as we walked between the barren trees behind the casket, it was as if it were yesterday that my aunt had said, "There shall we lie someday." Now we were placing her in the ground and the minister was saying the last words, "The Lord gave, and the Lord hath taken away; blessed be the name of the Lord."

It is hard to speak about death, particularly when one is close to it and it involves a beloved relative; but I have been thinking all week that there is no better time to consider one's death than when one is very much alive.

I appreciate why my aunt said what she said in Swedish. It is difficult to talk "out loud" about death, particularly about your own departure from this world. But if we are to approach death with quietness and calm, it helps if we bring it into the open.

In the lovely story of the Trapp Family Singers, one finds this thought weaving in and out of their lives, "God's will hath no why." That seems like a good starting point for living and dying, not to question God, not to challenge His appointments, even that final and sobering one — death.

The Almighty God who created us and put us into motion and keeps us in motion, surely He knows best when he wants to call us home again. God's will has no why. But this does involve a fine point with a rough edge.

Surely no one is going to die willingly if he hasn't lived yet, or if he hasn't lived right with God, or if he has an aching, cruel sorrow lodged deep in his heart, or if he is unreconciled with someone he loves. Then death comes too soon. Too soon.

As an older friend whispered to me from her bed in a hospital ward, "A good starting point for dying well is to live well."

Yes, to live well, to live close to God, and to accept His Word. Many of us read our Bibles as we read insurance policies — we get a sweeping impression, but skip the fine print.

In several places in the fine print God tells every man, not only the fallen ones, to pour out his heart to Him. King David's prayer for living and dying begins this way:

"Have mercy on me, O God."

There is wondrous, wide hope for all of us in God's great mercy. Without a doubt, God's clearest expression of mercy is found in His gift to us of His only Son. Isaiah describes Him well, "A man of sorrows, and acquainted with grief." Surely I can tell Him about my heartaches, my deep longings, my fears.

"There shall we lie someday." These words need not be stark and cold if we will consider the Man of sorrows. He alone takes the sting from death. He alone makes both living and dying pregnant with meaning.

Perhaps another reason my aunt spoke those solemn words that day in Swedish was an unconscious linking with the past — a thinking back to those happy days on the farm, but now so many have already gone on ahead, her mother and father, Aunt Hannah, her sister. Maybe her mind, already last summer when the grass was green, was getting in tune to join the others.

What a happy picture of heaven, a going home to God and loved ones. It is not hard to go someplace when you love and trust the people who are there.

"Där skall vi ligger en dag."

In the cold sod?
No, surely not.
A good shepherd does not leave his sheep out unattended. He leads them gently home. All the way home.
Spiritual Exercise: Read Psalms 13, 23 and 33.

7

NEVER STOP FORGIVING

Small Talk: I know two people who were once close friends. Some deep, incommunicable barrier was raised between them, and today they are going separate ways. Two people with the same faith, the same friends, the same work and the same interests, but going separately.

I no longer wonder why nations cannot get along, nations with different religions, different backgrounds, different goals, different colors, when friends who have everything in common cannot resolve their difficulties.

I do not know, nor do I care, what it was that caused the estrangement between these two good friends. Undoubtedly, in some measure, each was to blame. Rarely in brokenness is the fault on one side.

A short time after the break the younger of the two — I'll call him Mark — received insight into the wideness of God's forgiveness and the necessity of men to forgive one another. He went hopefully and joyfully to his friend.

But the thick, hard wall of partial forgiveness was already standing between them. He couldn't get through to his friend. His friend wasn't interested in reconciliation. He wanted to be left alone.

And Mark walked heavily away, a confused and tired man.

What a cruelly, hollow gesture is incomplete forgiveness that does not include the taking back of the contrite one!

There is only one way to forgive. The Bible portrays it in the story of the prodigal son. Here is a young man who breaks his father's heart as completely as it is possible to break a heart. When he finally comes to the end of himself and has no place to turn but home, he goes hoping his father will show mercy, even though he knows in his heart he deserves none.

As he approaches his father's property, he becomes more and more anxious — he thinks with deep shame of himself and he gets such a longing to have things made right. He knows he cannot stand it if his father is hard and icy toward him, yet in his heart he knows he deserves to be alienated forever and the tears in his eyes make it difficult for him to see. "But when he was yet a great way off, his father saw him . . . ." That thrills me. His father saw him. The one with forgiveness in his heart sees clearly. " . . . and had compassion, and ran, and fell on his neck, and kissed him."

This is true forgiveness.

And how beautiful. How beautiful.

And how rare.

After a year or so, Mark received a letter from his former friend. It was neither warm nor kind. It explained the long silence by saying, "I didn't know what to say."

No, there is nothing to say when we are not willing to take back those who have offended us. Had the father met his wayward son with cool reserve, they would never have had anything to say to one another either. It was only as they embraced each other and let their tears mingle that the festering hurt between them was cleansed and dissolved.

Forgiveness is extremely costly. It fairly tears out the heart of a man. It certainly breaks it, but it is in this brokenness of proud spirit and wounded heart that a man becomes truly melted by love. Gradually, some see it sooner than others, a man begins to see that the love of God in Christ is the greatest thing in the world, and that this love is manifested in forgiveness.

Peter once asked Christ, "How many times shall my brother sin against me and I forgive him?" I think Peter thought he was being very generous when he added, "Till seven times?"

Christ's answer must have staggered Peter as much as it does every man who lets these words sink in,

"I say not unto you, until seven times; but until seventy times seven."

In other words, there is never, no, never, a time when we are to stop forgiving one another. And how ironic — most of us haven't begun. Most of us, if our friends and relatives harass us three or four times, we're through. We've had it.

What a glad, free "Hallelujah" will ring out around the world the day we busy, important people truly humble ourselves before the Almighty God and before one another.

There is a way to patch up the sad, wide separations that come between proud people. It is the way of the cross. It has everything in the world, and in the world to come, to do with the word "forgive."

As we individuals grasp this, there will be marvelous flashes of brightness right in the neighborhood where we live. "See how those Christians love one another," our neighbors will say. "Surely their God is love, and we would know Him, too!"

Every time I ponder this truth, I get so hopeful that even I shall experience reconciliation with one of my lost friends. *Spiritual Exercise:* Repeat the Lord's Prayer.

8

THE INVITATION HAS BEEN SENT

Small Talk: "It is a great mistake my being born a man; I would have been much more successful as a sea gull or a fish." These words were spoken by Edmund in the play, "Long Day's Journey Into Night." Then Edmund goes on to say that he will always be a stranger who never feels at home, one who does not really want and is not really wanted, who can never belong. Even as a line in a dramatic performance that is a lonely, sad statement, but when you consider that Edmund is supposed to be a fairly true snapshot of the playwright himself, Eugene O'Neill, it piles heaviness on the words.

It is tragic to live life without hope. Life is a weight for everyone at times, but without a flicker of hope, the heaviness is unbearable; to always feel a stranger, to never belong. Obviously Edmund appreciated freedom — O to be a bird or a fish! *There* is lightness, *there is* escape; but not really. Sea gulls and fish die, and I believe that was Edmund's underlying tragic miscalculation. To state it simply, although there is nothing simple about it, Edmund thought the grave was the end. When I die, I die, was his philosophy.

I lived half of my life crouched under the weight of "When I die, I die," and so I know something about the suffocating quality of that philosophy. And all the time there is the Christ, always the same, yesterday, today, and forever, extending the loveliest invitation any of us will ever receive, "Come, come unto Me," and live.

It is the simplicity about the Christian faith that fools those who pride themselves in being "thinking" people. What kind of God says, "Come!" God should say, "Do!" or "Pay!" "Sacrifice!" or "Think!" That would make sense, but "Come!" — ridiculous. I cannot go along with a "simple" religion like this, the man of action says.

An intellectual recently said, "We are inveterate idol makers. . . . We make our God and put Him before us, and say, 'This is the way God ought to be.' Our pride is tenacious, even in religion. We become philosophical snobs instead of grateful adherents to God's great will."

What is amazing to everyone who simply accepts Christ's invitation to come is that He reveals Himself to that trusting person as God; but this occurs only after the believer has approached God in all simplicity and humility.

There are not adequate words to describe what a grand, glorious and hopeful thing it is to know that you belong to the Eternal God, and from the moment you thank the Saviour for inviting you, that dreadful "When I die, I die" is transformed into a lilting, happy "Because He lives, I live!"

Thomas Wolfe wrote in one of his books, "Which of us has not remained forever prison pent? Which of us is not forever a stranger and alone?" O, but Thomas Wolfe, there is a man who is not forever prison pent. There is a man who is not forever a stranger and alone. And Eugene O'Neill, there is a man who does feel at home, who knows he is wanted and is assured he belongs: this is the man, and it can be any man, every man, who kneels at the feet of his Saviour and whose very tears become a telescope with which he can catch a glimpse of the love of God. *Spiritual Exercise:* Read I Corinthians 15, the entire chapter, and ponder particularly verses 14, 34, and 54-58.

9

JANUARY DOLDRUMS AND THE REMEDY

Small Talk: One reason I have breakfast at the corner drugstore a couple of times each week, besides the fact they serve genuine, fresh orange juice (in living color), is that it is the only way I can get going in the morning. Of all the times in life when we need to stand together, it is in the morning, particularly the gray, cold, cheerless winter mornings in a large, lonely city.

By the time I hear the policemen and detectives, who come over from the Hudson Street Station, sputter, mutter, and laugh over their coffee about their common woes, by the time I watch Willie, the errand boy, slowly come to life and usefulness, by the time I exchange remarks with the pleasant, older woman who serves my breakfast, an understanding gets into my bones. I sense that I am not the only person who occasionally gets down, who wonders about the bewildering state this world is in, who is worn out by the holidays and depressed for no concrete reason other than a letdown feeling all over. As Ethel said when she brought the scrambled eggs and bacon, "I think January is the hardest month of all."

After she served me, and told the policemen if they wanted seconds on coffee, they knew where to get it (several years ago these chaps pinned a badge on Ethel for her outstanding service; they kid her unmercifully, and she loves it), she poured herself a cup and sat down at the table next to mine. "The thing I've noticed about myself," she continued, "I need to look forward to things. The months and days before Thanksgiving and Christmas are wonderful, because there is much to anticipate; then suddenly, it's over. And then if we're honest, we have to admit, the holidays were a little disappointing."

She laughed, "Perhaps if we wouldn't look at so much TV and stare at Christmas as celebrated on the covers of magazines, we'd think our modest celebrations were pretty nice. But that isn't the hardest part."

She was interrupted. The coffee pot needed filling. She came right back and went on, "No, the hardest part for me in January, I temporarily lose my sense of anticipation. Before Christmas, I was on a cloud. My son and his family were coming home, the first time in two years. Now they're gone, and you know what? I spent part of the week while they were here scolding the children. I thought they looked at TV too much, didn't hang up their coats; and then as if that wasn't enough, I picked on my son. I told him I thought he was working too hard, didn't spend enough time with his family."

I broke in, "If it will make you feel any better, that's just about the way I treated my family when I was home."

"Say, I've got to get to work, salad to cut up, more coffee to make, tables to set, and I've got to scoot these cops out of here." They gave her a menacing, affectionate look. As she gathered up her cup and saucer, she added, "Love is hard to express, but I think our families know we care for them, and that is the main thing."

As I walked out of the drugstore, I noticed in a display of paperbound books the title, *My Fight for Sanity*. It struck me that that is not one man's story or one woman's story. It is every man's story today as this rocking and tense age hurls forward. Is there any hope for us?

Yes, I'll say there is hope, and often right along the line of this simple drugstore scene we get a glimmer of an answer. It is in this almost naive sharing, laughing, kidding which goes on among people as they gather in cafes, drop in on neighbors for a cup of coffee, take time to chat with one another. It is in this casual person-to-person, friend-to-friend meeting that one often picks up little packets of hope, just enough to keep going on for another twenty-four hours. There is a plus feature about hope, too. I don't know if you've noticed it, but whenever you have hope, it is generally accompanied by the ineffable combination of inner quietness and outer usefulness which is simply another way of saying that you enjoy sound mental health.

But there is far more to hope than communicating with others, as valuable and necessary as that is; something more is needed. Laughing, joking, sharing, and being friendly only reach the horizontal in us, or at least in me. I need the mountain peaks of Holy Scripture to reach to the depths of my inadequacy, lostness, and occasional real battles with hopelessness. I need to be forcefully reminded on a gray, cheerless January day as I walk up Clark Street amid dirt and noise (as Frank Lloyd Wright once said, "Is anything uglier than just dirt, unless it is noise? We have both in abundance.") that "The counsel of the Lord standeth forever, the thoughts of his heart to all generations."

And it interests me how often a letter can bring into flame this hope we so desperately need to keep us going on the gloomy days, like this note I received from Switzerland. I have two American friends, about the nicest people I know (and I know a lot of nice people), who are in charge of a home for handicapped children in the Swiss mountains near Montreux. When I visited them about two years ago, they had just made a down payment on a large, four-story chalet, ideal for their work, but a gigantic undertaking for two women. However, they never thought of themselves as being "alone" in this venture of devotion. Theirs is that uncomplicated faith which hopes and dares the impossible, because they honestly believe God would have them do this work.

Now they have fifteen patients and several other helpers, although they could use more help. It takes three of them a couple of hours to dress and feed one child. Ann and Mary in helping these children are remembering that their twisted, ill-functioning bodies also have souls.

The youngest child, two-year-old Danny, a dear blond lad from Basel, is now learning to sit alone and is even beginning to stand with very little support. Danny and his pal, Jean-Jacques, four, also greatly handicapped physically, were found recently on a balcony which looks out on a majestic alpine landscape which outshines any painting or post card you might have seen of Switzerland, and there they were sitting with their small hands folded, Jean-Jacques praying in French and Danny in German.

"Dear Father, thank You, thank You, thank You."

The January doldrums are like malaria, generally intermittent and recurrent. I had a slight fever the beginning of the month, then had a complete and happy recovery, only to have another attack last night. January is such a long month. The fact that a person is not consistently "abounding in hope," cheerful and courageous to the end, does that nullify the words of faith spoken in this Book? No, I think rather it strengthens the real picture of what the Christian life is. It reminds me that no one attains a certain stature in the Christian life. Whether we are ministers, bishops, carpenters, teachers, writers, speakers, housewives, businessmen, a loyal church worker for sixty-five years, none of us have attained a higher rank. It is as one good man said, "A stumbling forward," and may I add, the Christian life is a continual reaching up and out, and underneath are the everlasting arms of the only wise God our Saviour.

Spiritual Exercise: "When you cannot stand," St. Francis de Sales wrote, "He will bear you in His arms. Do not look forward to what may happen tomorrow; the same everlasting Father who cares for you today, will take care of you tomorrow, and every day .... Be at peace then, and put aside all anxious thoughts and imaginations." This is the prayer for all those who have momentarily lost hope: "Dear Lord, help me to put aside all anxious thoughts and imaginations, and give me Thy peace so I might be hopeful again." Read Revelation, chapter 22.

10

WHAT'S THE MATTER WITH YOU?

Small Talk: I like to drop in at my house once in awhile. Mostly because I love the people who live there. Also, you never know who you're going to meet.

When I walked into the kitchen the other day, I had to detour around a wisp of a child seated on the floor painting in a color book.

"Hello," I said. "Who are you?"

Without looking up from her painting, she stated,

"I'm Marcie, of course."

"Of course, you're Marcie," I replied. "I'm glad to meet you. By the way, Marcie, where are the others? You know, those who live here?"

"Some are up, and some down."

By this time those who were down came rushing up. We jigged around noisily for a few minutes, but not Marcie. She sat painting purple cows. Soon my niece and nephew joined her.

I walked over to get a drink of water before hunting the other members of the family. I saw my vitamin bottle on the ledge, so popped a tablet in my mouth. Just as I did this, the silent painter of purple cows lifted her tiny head, looked me smack in the eye, and said,

"What's the matter with you?"

I'll never be able to take *anything* again without hearing that puncturing declamation, "What's the matter with you?"

The way most of us adults plow through life, it would be more to the point to ask, "What isn't the matter with you?"

We have so many aches and pains and troubles there is scarcely time left to talk about anything else. We adults past 35 tend to take ourselves too seriously. I know I do, and every time I do, I bog down quickly. Then the Lord sends me a Marcie. Three cheers for these little ones who have a way of making us see ourselves as we really are. Not what we're pretending to be.

If you are an adult who is living in a world without children, you are the loser. The nice part about children, they seem to be all over. You don't have to have your own. You can stumble over them in the oddest places.

I particularly need to have Marcie ask me every once in awhile, "What's the matter with you?" to remind me that anyone who has it as good as I do hasn't the right to have anything the matter with her. "This is the day the Lord hath made . . ." I *will* rejoice and be glad in it.

A friend of mine and one of the most relaxed, happy men I know, was telling me the other day,

"I've been losing my hair gradually for ten years. It isn't a bit noticeable to me if I look at myself in the mirror from a certain angle. So I've been pretty much seeing myself as I was ten years ago. That is, until my four-year-old daughter gave me a rude awakening.

"One night I took my family out to dinner. While I parked the car I told them to go ahead in the cafeteria line. By the time I came in, they were already seated. The children were playing a game, seeing who could spot me first.

"Our youngest daughter shouted, 'There he is.'

"My wife turned to look, 'No, that's not Daddy.'

"'But mother,' she said loudly, 'he's got a hole in his head just like Daddy!'"

And how — children have a way of making us see ourselves as we are! People who are growing older with aches in our bones and holes in our heads.

The wise man is the one who accepts himself as he is, where he is, and how he is, and lives his life knowing "this is the day the Lord hath made . . ." and tries, in spite of all his limitations and frustrations, to " . . . rejoice and be glad in it."

And when he does, it is as the song writer said, "Walk on, walk on, with hope in your heart, and you'll never walk alone."

Spiritual Exercise: If you do not already own one, walk to the nearest book store and pick up one or two paperbound gospel hymnbooks. Return to your room. Either standing or sitting, alone or in a group, pick out several of the happiest of the hymns, and let yourself go.

PART 3

To the End

11

NEVER WILL I FORGET IT

Small Talk: The other evening when I was reading my favorite devotional book, *Daily Strength for Daily Needs,* I came on this red-lettered notation which I had made a year ago: "Never will I forget this day as long as I live!" I re-read it several times. Hard as I could think with my middle-aged brain, I could not remember what it was that I will never forget as long as I live.

You may laugh at me. Go ahead. I laughed myself. You see what I mean? It is easy to take yourself too seriously. To think your sorrows the greatest, your problems the thorniest, your circumstances the most complex. Then, happily, something ridiculous like this happens, and suddenly the picture is in focus.

Whatever it was that I was moaning about last year had been crowded out of my mind by happy, good experiences. As the psalmist said, "Weeping may endure for a night, but joy cometh in the morning."

Such a lovely promise, because who hasn't had his night of weeping? They come, and they will come again, but how refreshing to know that later on, with the dawn — possibly the dawn of the next day, but more likely the dawn of the next month or year — joy will steal in. God does not always move in His joy swiftly; but eventually the joy comes again. Of this I am certain, and it helps to keep alive a quiet smile while waiting, *if* we will remember this.

A night or two after I had written, "Never will I forget this day as long as I live!" I had copied down, also in red pencil, this dreary remark, "We are in the world to suffer and die."

Truly I must have been going through something those days

to derive comfort from the dismal thought we are in the world exclusively to suffer and die!

In all honesty, I believe there is more to life than suffering and dying. One of the curious things about life, it is hard to pin down. The minute you put it into words, as this missionary, you can easily miss the mark. His remark is true as far as it goes. Most of us past thirty-five have already acquainted ourselves with the naked truth that there is suffering and dying in living. But to say this is life! I cannot go along. My own experience has taught me otherwise. Joy is real, and I can say the same words David said from a joyful heart which knew many tears, "O Lord my God, I will give thanks unto thee for ever."

How strange life is, because some, often quite a bit, of our thankfulness to God relates to the suffering. When all is easy and prosperous, it is easy to put God in a back room. Quite a few of us who are "prone to wander" have found our way back to our Lord through suffering.

It just came to me, what it was that I will never forget as long as I live! I won't tell you what it was. It wouldn't be important to you, and as I turn the thing around in my mind, I find it isn't very important to me either.

In talking about some of the ingredients a person needs to live life to the end, some friends and I threw these in the mixing bowl: the human spirit needs a settled faith in the one, true God, at the same time maintaining a questing mind; he needs quite a bit of love; a strong sense of purpose; a grasp on the little known fact that he is in the world to serve; and to really "live it up" to the end, it doesn't harm a man to be somewhat of a clown once in awhile. As a man who is renowned for his wisdom said, "To every thing there is a season ... a time to weep, and a time to laugh; a time to mourn, and a time to dance ... I know that there is no good in them, but for a man to rejoice, and to do good in his life." *Spiritual Exercise:* Take a closer look at the weights in your life. Could any of them be lightened by taking a lighter approach? Be honest. I think too many of us enjoy our "suffering" too much. Study Colossians 1:9-29 and Philippians 3:13, 14.

12

PANCAKE SUPPERS

Small Talk: The other day I was thinking how strongly I am influenced by the things other people say. I understand better now why I am driven nearly out of my mind by commercials and much of the advertising in this present chaotic age.

I have a regrettable habit of listening. Most people have some sort of built-in mechanism which filters out what they don't want to hear, or at least they must have. How else can you explain why there isn't an organized campaign against huckstering?

As Adlai Stevenson said, "With the supermarket as our temple and the singing commercial as our litany, are we likely to fire the world with an irresistible vision of America's exalted purposes and inspiring way of life?"

I keep wondering what children are going to say about their fathers thirty and forty years from now. About the best some of them will be able to say, "I can see my father now, stretched out in his contour chair watching TV."

Happily there are still some among us who have exalted purposes and live inspiring lives, like the late Grandma Moses, for example. "If I hadn't started painting, I would have raised chickens," she told someone who asked her what made her become an artist at the age many people hardly have strength left to rock.

"I could still do it now." She was talking about the chickens. "I would never sit back in a rocking chair, waiting for someone to help me. I have often said, before I would call for help from outsiders, I would rent a room in the city some place and give pancake suppers, just pancakes and syrup, and they could have water, like a little breakfast."

It is not all loss when you are the listener. Even if you stumble on to one gem like this every other year, it makes you glad you were listening.

I'm thankful to Grandma Moses for that pancake idea. Living doesn't interest me in the least if it does not have an element of fun in it. Somehow it strikes me as a delightful idea to wind up one's days in a rented room giving pancake suppers. First thing though, I must learn how to make Swedish pancakes. I've been meaning to get this recipe from my mother for 25 years, but you know how it is, these things slip the mind. But now that it involves my old age, I'm bearing down.

It is not easy to get these recipes. Years ago I tried to put down my grandmother's recipe for rye bread. "Well," she said, "I take flour and butter, and of course," she smiled, "I always add a little cream." Not once did she say exactly what went into it, and so when I tried to make the bread I had to guess at what she meant by a pinchful of this or a shake of that. Sad to relate, no one else in the family was any wiser than I. When Grandma Carlson went home to be with the Lord, the secret of her delicious homemade bread was locked in her heart.

One thing about listening to others, you don't have to do everything they say. I'm sure Grandma Moses won't mind, but at my pancake suppers, I'm serving steaming cups of amber coffee. Egg coffee, I already know how to make that.

Open a fresh can of coffee. Measure out several tablespoons of coffee into the pot. Take a raw egg and mix coffee and egg together. Boil water separately and pour on mixture. Bring to boil again, stirring a little.

If the phone rings, and it boils over, don't feel badly. For some reason, boiled-over coffee tastes better. Clean stove while coffee is settling. Then pour out in cups in a room where the sun is shining through polished windows with geraniums on the window sill.

When you bring in the platters of hot, buttered, golden-edged Swedish pancakes served with lingon berries, something tells me, the people will come. They'll come. You'll need no singing commercial, no neon sign.

Spiritual Exercise: With feet close together bend from the waist, reach out right hand and turn off the TV set. In comfortable sitting position, read Ecclesiastes, chapter three.

13

TAKE AN AIR OF DETACHMENT

Small Talk: Last night I was going through a stack of music accumulated over the years, and the French song, "Ne pas perdre la tete," turned up.

"Ne pas perdre la tete" (Don't lose your head) was popular in Europe many years ago. Roughly it goes like this: "Don't ever lose your head. You should never get irritated or boil over. Whenever something provokes you, simply take an attitude of detachment."

Believe me, that is a rough translation. The whole thing sounds much better in French, but no matter how you say it, that "air of detachment" is worth having. I'm embroiled in a couple of situations right now where the furrows on my brow could be gentler if I could "prenez un air detaché."

Different men arrive at their states of detachment in different ways. This past week I have been re-acquainting myself with two authors I read with enthusiasm in my youthful days.

Philip, the main character in Somerset Maugham's masterpiece, *Of Human Bondage,* arrives at his air of detachment by concluding that life has no meaning. From his birth Philip experienced nothing but pain, disease and unhappiness. All the bright hopes of his youth dissolved. His vicar uncle, a Pharisee of the Pharisees, turned Philip with loathing from the Bible, because his young mind assumed it was in that Book his uncle had learned his false and cruel way of life. Finally Philip becomes totally disillusioned with everyone and everything, and his soul cries out, "What is the use of it?" What is the use of life? Suddenly he decides that there is no meaning in life, and man by living serves no end. Philip decides that it is immaterial whether a man is born or not born, whether he lives or ceases to live. Life, he concludes, is insignificant and death has no consequence.

For the first time Philip feels free, for if life is meaningless, the world is robbed of its cruelty. What he does with his life or what he leaves undone does not matter. Failure is unimportant and success amounts to nothing. He, Philip, is the most inconsiderate creature on earth and at the same time almighty, because he has wrenched from chaos the secret of its nothingness.

So much for Philip and his "air of detachment."

Another man who wrote a best seller arrived at his freedom along these lines. In his words, his philosophy goes like this: "...forsake this wretched world, and your soul shall find rest. Learn to despise outward things, and to give yourself to things inward, and you shall perceive the kingdom of God to come in you." Then he talks about the inadvisability of trusting men, "They that today are with you, tomorrow may be against you; and often again they turn around like the wind."

That is Thomas á Kempis speaking, and his book, *The Imitation of Christ,* has been for five hundred years the most widely read book of devotions in the world. It is not known how many editions have appeared in the various languages into which this great classic has been translated since the first Latin printing was issued at Augsburg in 1486.

To me this is a tremendous commentary on how desperately man has longed to find a haven in the tempest of living.

I am arriving at my "air of detachment" somewhere in between these two outlooks on life.

More power to Philip if he can "draw long breaths of joyous satisfaction" by believing there is no meaning in life. However, everything I have heard, learned, and experienced convinces me that God works for good in everything with those who love Him and are called according to His purpose.

His purpose.

I rejoice in the knowledge that God has purpose.

If I believed that life had no purpose, I could never, never "draw long breaths of joyous satisfaction" as Philip. I'd be far more inclined to take an overdose of sleeping tablets.

On the other hand, I cannot seem to stretch my neck as far as Thomas á Kempis and live so completely in heavenly places that I arrive at detachment by scorning the things of earth.

I'll admit that there are times when this appeals to me. Who isn't familiar with the feeling, "The world is too much with me"? But Holy Scripture does not say, "God so loved this *wretched* world that he gave..." Not at all. We're simply told that God so loved the world that He gave His only Son that whoever believes in Him should not perish but have eternal life.

He is my bedrock for the detached air: a simple trust in the loving Saviour. Even on my most mixed-up days, there is great gain in remembering that He is with me always — even until the end. And He walks with every man on earth who dares to trust Him.

As for the inadvisability of trusting men, I cannot go along with you, Thomas á Kempis. You have written many fine things, but here we differ sharply.

It is quite possible that God does speak with those who dwell in closets. Even a simple woman like myself has known the wonder of God speaking to her in a quiet, secluded place; but more often God has spoken to me while I have been brushing elbows on a crowded sidewalk, visiting a sick friend at midnight or on a canoe trip with friends along the Gun Flint Trail.

I doubt seriously that if a person has never learned to trust a friend he will ever have great confidence in God. It is quite popular among "the religious" to pray for others, to walk through prisons and hospitals passing out literature, etc. But I dare say one letter or visit to someone you're concerned about is equal to twenty prayers; and to pause and listen to one lonely soul in a hospital ward is better than all the printed words in the world.

Do not misunderstand me. I believe in prayer. I believe in printed words. I wouldn't have written this book if I didn't believe it was possible to communicate warm, living thoughts through the medium of cold, motionless words; but we must never lose the picture of Jesus walking among men, taking children in His arms, visiting with His friends.

As that truthful Bonhoeffer once said, "We ought not to try and be more religious than God Himself."

Spiritual Exercise: Sing softly "Jesus Calls Us O'er the Tumult." Sometime between this sundown and the next, go call on someone, anyone, who might be glad to see *you*. And if you are confined to a room, let us pray that the Spirit will enlighten your mind on how you might reach out to someone even from that bed.

14

NEVER THE SAME

Small Talk: If you do not mind, I should like to share with you one of the first articles I wrote. At that time I lived in a tiny beach house leaning over the edge of Lake Minnetonka. The Lord had put me in this place away from everything for awhile to teach me certain things. I am most certain I did not learn all my lessons, but this one thing I did get. Surely it is one of the grandest truths. James expressed it this way, "Draw nigh to God, and he will draw nigh to you."

I don't know where we get the idea that if we seek God's presence it is going to be the end of laughter in our lives. I do not know when I had such good times as I had those three years in that snug little house perched above one of Minnesota's ten thousand lakes. God seemed in everything. He was. I saw Him in the storms that raged across the lake, and on those marvelously still evenings when the moonlight made my lake into a gigantic crown of tiny twinkling diamonds, there was God. When He threw snow down from His sky, I didn't mind. Not at all. It only made me more mindful of His presence. I'll never forget when those daffodils peeked out on the bank just outside my window. I thought I had never seen anything so happy. Simply God smiling again.

I'll never forget those years. Here is the column.

> *Spring Park, Minnesota*
> *October 1956*
> *I was listening to "The Farm Hour" this morning. Not completely by choice. What else is there to listen to at 5:30 in the morning?*
> *A person who lives alone, sooner or later, works out a little routine. I have found out that while fixing and eating breakfast it is a friendly thing to have the radio on. Not only friendly, but educational.*
> *Did you know that cows have multiple stomachs? I never knew this. No one ever told me. And I surely never thought to*

ask. So with my second cup of coffee I did some research. Not that I really doubted the announcer, but. . . .

I'm a bit handicapped with my encyclopedia set. It goes only to Volume 8 (EDUC-EXPL). I started collecting the books last year at the Minnetonka Supermarket, and then left town for a few months after Volume 8 had been carried home with the hamburger and peanut butter. Now the supermarket is giving away Buicks and Cadillacs. I'll never know what gives from F to Z.

But it is surprising and satisfying how much of interest there is in life from A to F. And so in this research problem I did the direct thing, I looked up "cows." But encyclopedias are like telephone directories, things are never under what you think they should be; but these editors are not unfeeling men. They take into consideration there will be a few of us who think cows should be discussed under "cows" and will look here first, and they give directions. The little notice states I was to look under "cattle," happily still within my range. After all, they could have thrown them into the section on "the fauna and flora of North America."

So I looked up "cattle," and true, the encyclopedia backed up the announcer. I really wasn't doubting the announcer, but it was pretty early in the morning.

So cows have four stomachs. As the Supermarket encyclopedia stated it, "A cow is an animal which has a four-compartmental stomach." This perhaps could explain the cow's look of contentment. Recently since I've been doing my own cooking, I've had the feeling I could look more contented if I had an extra stomach or two.

After the cows, my announcer friend on "The Farm Hour" got started on pigs. As if he hadn't given me enough to think about for one morning. Above my rattling of dishes in the kitchen, I heard him say in the same smooth voice announcers use to talk about hand lotion or baby powder, ". . . and it's the same with pigs as people."

I stopped rattling, and listened. He went on to describe a wonderworking drug which could completely change the lives of pigs. Never have pigs had it so good, I gathered. So I decided to research this theory that it is the same with pigs as people.

This time I had to go to the library. The trip was rewarding. I found a Sven Lidman of Sweden who has written a whole essay on pigs and people. Mr. Lidman points out that what interests most people is what interests pigs: food, warmth, sleep, sex, security.

I don't know why I should be surprised. Surely thousands of people are exerting every ounce of their intelligence exploiting this fact. Look at much of our "literature" today. Absolutely geared to our "piggy interests." But why single out literature? The majority of our movies, current plays, the advertising we are exposed to day and night, all going great guns because these promoters are operating on the principle that it's the same with people as pigs.

And the church hasn't escaped. A well-known missionary recently said concerning certain of the promotion schemes used by some ministers:

"It has come to the stage where seminaries should require their students to have six months with Barnum and Bailey and another six at Tammany Hall before they send them out to be ministers!"

This is all rather strange to find so many content to live on this level where it's the same with pigs as people when the great fundamental revelation of time and eternity regarding the entire race is that God has redeemed us. Any man or woman who acts on the fact that Christ died for him or her, from this moment forward, can never be the same. Christ always lifts up.

Spiritual Exercise: Ponder anew these mysterious, marvelous, almost unbelievable words: "Draw nigh to God, and he will draw nigh to you."

15

TO THE END OF THE WORLD

Small Talk: As we came down the hill from Monterey, the moment we saw the sloping, sugar-white beach and the magnificent blue Pacific, I started kicking off my shoes. My friend, Nancy, was driving, but by the time the car stopped, she had her shoes off, too, and we raced through the sand to the icy water.

There is an indescribable something about Carmel that exhilarates. This was not the first time Nancy and I had run on the white sands of Carmel.

Later as we sat on a sand dune to catch our breath, we remarked that we had been in better condition the last time we had tried to outrun the breakers at Carmel. Nancy and I had met years ago when we were stationed at the desert outpost, Camp Elliott, a few hundred miles south of Carmel. If the Navy hadn't done anything else for us, it had put us in top condition physically; I'm not so sure mentally. Nancy had come to Elliott from Hunter College where she had done everything short of pulling a battle ship behind her while jumping through a hoop to qualify as a Specialist First Class. I had arrived in a state of preparedness to win the war singlehandedly from the Yeoman Training Center in Stillwater, Oklahoma.

We were so keyed up for "action" when we mustered in at Camp Elliot, had they issued the directive that either of us were to replace the Commandant, we would have given a salute and taken over.

But no one asked us to assume command of the station. In fact, few at Elliott had heard of WAVES. It strained their military ingenuity thinking of jobs for us to do.

I am not positive, but I think it was in the scullery where Nancy and I first met. I was assigned to pots, and she was on pans. Or it might have been on that cleaning detail where we walked around with long, pointed sticks. They were rugged, wild and funny years, and those of us who shared the experience have a get together now and then and laugh.

And Nancy and I did talk and laugh, and then we grew silent as we watched the sun explode into the ocean scattering pinks and lavenders and red shadows across the waves. As we stood up to go and started up the hill, a full, white moon had just come over the blue hills. As I said, you cannot describe Carmel.

We started hunting a room near the ocean. Found one, and a shuffling old lady escorted us to it. We really didn't want the room when we saw it, but felt sorry for the woman, and took it. She was over ninety, going blind, had had several strokes, and her daughter told us was feeling extra badly because the neighbor across the street had died that morning. The old lady kept asking us, "Why couldn't it have been me?"

I haven't been able to shake that question, "Why couldn't it have been me?'" I have heard it before. Not only do old people ask it, but sick people, tired people, people who have given up, people who have lost their zest for living.

I wonder, though, if this is honoring to God?

Didn't our Lord tell us that He would be with us to the end of the world?

It is possible that some of us need to ask God to renew our spirits and sharpen our awareness that if we are still here, we are here for a reason. God can use a broken, tired and aged vessel to glow through. He does not need youth and vitality to demonstrate His grace.

My mother found this verse encircled in the Bible of an aunt whom we had all loved and enjoyed and who had maintained a delightful sense of humor and an inner spiritual force and a love for people to the end; she was Auntie Hannah to more people than our immediate family: "Now also when I am old and grey-headed, O God, forsake me not; until I have shewed thy strength unto this generation, and thy power to every one that is to come."

Thank you, dear faithful one, you showed it to many of us.

Whatever our weaknesses and infirmities, God can yet be glorified through you and me, if we look to Him and reflect His glorious light. The prophet, Micah, had his troubles too, but nevertheless he wrote,

"When I sit in darkness, the Lord shall be a light unto me."

Spiritual Exercise: Either sitting or kneeling, ask God to give you grace to follow Him all the days of your life, and most of all, grace for this moment. It is best not to get too far ahead. It is well to know the Lord is here now.

Read Psalm 61 and Psalm 71.

16

BUT AFTER THIS

Small Talk: When I was walking this morning, a fine, brisk, sunny morning, I almost bumped into a man coming around the corner on North Avenue. He was lining up cars for a funeral procession. First in line was the long, open car piled high with flowers, then the glossy, gray hearse, followed by ten or twelve cars. Please do not think I was standing and staring, but there it was and there I was.

And there were others who became innocently involved in this private, solemn moment. Usually when I pass the meat market, Pete the meatman waves at me, but today he was lining up his sausages and weiners with a faraway look on his face. He must see many funerals, because his shop is in the same block with the mortuary; but shopkeepers, clerks, authors, housewives, and policemen never learn to take death in stride. We all viewed it with wonder, respect and awe, and some, fear.

Have you noticed, there are no cartoons about death? Those who like to make others laugh have invaded every other sacred and profane experience common to man, but as a psychologist said, "So awful is bereavement to human beings that it is the only emotional area in which no amusing cartoons seem to exist."

This funeral procession made me think of three people.

First, a friend of mine, a remarkable woman in her eighties, who hasn't been out of her apartment in years. She sits by her window in a dreary, dumpy apartment on the second floor, and she, too, has a funeral procession to watch nearly every day, as she lives across the street from the mortuary.

She told me one afternoon when I had stopped by for a cup of coffee, "Some people might find this morbid, to watch so many funerals, but I learn a lot about people as I look from this window." She bent forward and picked up the worn Bible from the cluttered table, "And it only makes the words in here more precious."

She said very simply, "We're all going to die, you know." She handed me the Bible, "Would you read Hebrews, chapter nine? I can't see the print very well any more."

I looked it up and read the chapter. When I got to the end, she asked me to repeat the last two verses, "And as it is appointed unto men once to die, but after this the judgment: So Christ was once offered to bear the sins of many, and unto them that look for him shall he appear the second time without sin unto salvation."

She said, "That part about 'But after this . . .' — do you ever think about that?" But before I could answer, she said gently, "I love the last part of the message — '. . . and unto them that look for him . . . .'" Then she paused and said these last words slowly and with a majestic swell, "He shall appear!" Suddenly I was no longer in a drab, sad flat in one of Chicago's less appealing neighborhoods, but I saw it as my friend did, as good a place as any to await this solemn, holy appointment with God.

Then I thought about that great Scotsman, Samuel Rutherford, who was one of the most eloquent preachers of the seventeenth century. He wrote in a letter to a good friend, "Remember how swiftly God's post time flieth away; and that your forenoon is already spent, your afternoon will come, and then your evening, and at last night, when ye cannot see to work. Let your heart be set upon finishing of your journey and summing and laying your accounts with your Lord. Oh, how blessed shall ye be to have a joyful welcome of your Lord at night! How blessed are they who, in time, take sure course with their souls!"

And this funeral procession brought to my mind a third person, a fellow newspaper columnist, Odd McIntyre. He was telling in one of his columns about a Sunday night when he and a friend, not regular church-goers, passed a small church and decided to enter.

He commented how he could not help but reflect on the thousands of churches similarly struggling — veritable vortexes in the gathering storms. Each trying valiantly and often pathetically to establish a need of hope, peace and comfort in a hungering world of vanishing faith. And then he remarked how little most of us help in such worthy endeavor.

Also he said something about the fact that he had had a particularly troubling week, and yet when he left the small church he felt peaceful and had a fresh clarity of thought and vision about the week to come, but "like so many laggards," he concluded, "it will probably be some time before I go to church again."

Another columnist, known for his crisp language, added this postscript to the story, "Curiously, Odd McIntyre was wrong in his last estimate. He was back in church in a flower-draped casket just days later."

Spiritual Exercise: May we do what my good friend suggested, think about the words in those two arresting verses, particularly, "But after this . . ."

PART 4

Laughingly, Tearfully, and Faithfully

*The fruit of the Spirit is love, joy, peace,
longsuffering, gentleness, goodness, faith,
meekness, temperance.*—Galatians 5:22,23

17

A SMILE HELPS

Small Talk: Yesterday I received a letter from a friend who is
"fighting the battle of life" in a large city. Jean has more than
her share of grievances — not ordinary, neat problems that one
can wrap up and send out of one's life, but the kind that don't
fit in packages and you just have to live with them cluttering up
your life.

She shared with me in this letter only one of the woes. It
read like a chapter from a Dostoevsky novel, but once she had
aired it, she was back in her usual "you might as well laugh as cry"
mood, and finished her letter with this bit of nonsense: "And
now that I have adjusted to another of life's little situations, let
us say farewell to beautiful Hawaii and go off into the sunset."

Anyone with a sense of humor cannot stay down long.
When I read that foolish (but wonderful) sentence after her
tale of doom, it gave me the assurance that she was going to
make it, in spite of this latest blow.

No one can deny that her life is a hard one, but so is mine
and so are the lives of everyone on earth. The very people we
think have the least in the way of worries often have the most.
Eliphaz, in the book of Job, put it this way: "Although affliction
cometh not forth of the dust, neither doth trouble spring out of
the ground; yet man is born unto trouble, as the sparks fly
upward."

I know some people whose lives are a veritable Fourth of July, but none of us are spared some flying sparks, a few Roman candles. If we're going to survive, we need to put on fireproof garments to insulate us against the flying sparks. And humor is one of these garments.

I must clarify one point though. I could not possibly rejoice over the fact that Jean had been able to momentarily rise above this latest pile of trouble dumped upon her, if I did not know a few years ago she made a basic commitment. Her God is my God, "Though he slay me, yet will I trust him." And Job's God.

Why God doesn't take away all of our burdens, why He hasn't removed your heartache and mine, is the mystery of all ages. But I am slowly learning that God does behold our sufferings with an eye of mercy, and He alone is able to uphold us in the midst of the sparks flying, and even to use the trouble for our good.

A friend is not much of a friend if he is not willing to accept all of you, your sorrows as well as your joys; but it is not fair to use friends as wailing walls and never inject a bit of hope or cheer into what you write. The best thing is to pray before you write. As Melancthon wrote in the troublesome days of the sixteenth century, "Trouble and perplexity drive us to prayer, and prayer driveth away trouble and perplexity."

Spiritual Exercise: Be very conscious of the next ten letters you write to be sure you put in something cheerful and hopeful.

18

MISTAKES I HAVE MADE

Small Talk: In the magazine, *Progressive Farmer,* there is a column called, "Mistakes I Have Made." Here farmers and farmers' wives share their mistakes, I suppose, with the idea that one can learn from another person's errors.

A farmer from Georgia wrote, "One of my good brood sows got sick." (What followed was in farmer language and I know nothing about farming — but what he said next made a lot of sense.) "I paid little attention. Soon eleven pigs showed the same symptoms. Before I realized I should do something about it, they were all dead. If I had devoted more time to the physical condition of my hogs, this wouldn't have happened."

If I were a farmer, I'd have nine or ten letters in that column every month.

When it comes to mistakes I have made, I stand tall among my fellow creatures. To be sure, I haven't let any pigs die through my lack of devotion, but only because I don't have pigs.

If this were a sermon (and it surely is not), I'd take as my text three passages from the farmer's letter: "I paid little attention . . . ," "Before I realized . . . ." and "If I had . . . ."

As I enter this challenging era known as "Life Begins at Forty," I find I am almost strangled by the trilogy: "I paid little attention . . . ," "Before I realized . . . ," "If I had . . . ."

Last year I decided to take a job for awhile. I thought the experience would do me good, and I looked forward to being out among people, and if they were going to give me one of those nice envelopes every month, I wasn't going to turn it down. Columnists like to pay their bills, too.

But I cannot tell you how many friends told me not to go to work. They said, you'll never have time for your writing.

I paid little attention.

I took the job, and *before I realized it,* I was finding it difficult even to get an article a month written. I finally gave up the writing altogether. I needed every ounce of bounce I had to make it through the day. I was working as a librarian — no, that's not right, I was *the* librarian in a junior high school. For the past fifteen or twenty years I have been taking children and teen-agers one or two at a time, but you place eight hundred in one building . . . !!!

If I had only listened! But, no, I'm glad I didn't. Now that I have lived through it, I'm most grateful for that year as a school librarian. I entered into a whole new and deep appreciation for the teachers of our country. The school I worked in was in sad shape, but the teachers weren't. There were several on that one staff who were as visionary, inspiring, and dedicated as some of the grand teachers I had when I went to school, who taught me that life will never let down the child who keeps alive in his heart a sense of wonder and thanksgiving.

Spiritual Exercise: I think where many of us get tripped up in life is in our attitude. We act as if someone handed us a brochure when we were born informing us that we are now entering this little adventure known as life, and it will be sunshine and sweetness, ease and comfort, and if we'll just sit back, all the good things will come to us. This is so far from truth that about all we can do about it is laugh. Quite a few cry, and that is all right for a short season; then it's best to smile and ask God: "What can I do, Lord, to make the town in which I live a better place? What can I do to show that I love Thee?"

19

BE GONE, DULL CARE

Small Talk: While typing the junior high film schedule for next year, I was reminded how difficult it is in life to have things come at the right time. Education, for example. Many of the youngsters in this school couldn't care less about "The Family Budget," "Percent in Everyday Life," or "The Digestive System of the Human Body." These are all films they are going to see next year; but I know hundreds of furrow-browed parents who would give anything to know more about the family budget, particularly how to live within it.

Then digestion. The peak of interest in digestion comes later. It is at club meetings and on the golf course that one talks about the duodenum and the gall bladder. And percent in life? Who are those vitally interested in percentages? The school teacher or plumber who has five shares of International Packers, or the widow figuring her church tithe based on her income from Social Security and the two rooms she rents, or me and my income tax.

I would love to return to Benton Harbor next year as a student. Nearly everything they are teaching I need to know. Just seeing the films on this schedule would be enlightening.

We're starting in September with an art film called, "Be Gone, Dull Care." Just saying that title over does something therapeutic for me. *Be gone, dull care. Be gone. Be gone.*

Most of us adults gather sufficient fortitude and courage to meet the whirlwinds in our lives, but the small, dull cares — these are our undoing. They make us grouches. In short, they drug us and eventually kill our spirit unless — unless we learn to pray them away, laugh them away, sing them away.

Be Gone, Dull Care.

Gone.

Gone.

So our ears can hear the creation song which is raised every morning at our doorstep. So we may respond to the drama of life with joyous laughter and sympathetic tears.

A big fault in education today is that we are not educating enough eccentrics. Eccentrics like Milton who say in one sentence what lesser men pour into volumes,

"The end of all learning is to know God, and out of that knowledge to love and imitate him."

Spiritual Exercise: Read Proverbs Chapter 8 and John 1:1-14.

20

THE MIDDLE CHILD

Small Talk: When we were small, my brothers, sister and I loved to have our mother tell us about when she was twelve and went to Sweden. We loved this story better than the *Wizard of*

Oz. We had her tell it over and over. It always sounded freshly exciting.

It always was freshly exciting.

The story began at the moment Mother met Nancy, another bright-eyed twelve-year-old farm girl traveling with her parents to Denmark. Invariably we'd interrupt mother to have her explain again why she was chosen to go with Grandma.

You see — she would explain — Grandpa knew how much it meant to Grandma to go home once more to see her father and the homeland, and so for years he secretly saved for this trip to Sweden.

Then the problem arose, who should go with Grandma? He couldn't. There were nine children to look after and horses and pigs and lambs and chickens. Crops to be gathered in. The two older daughters couldn't go. They were needed to bake and clean and mend and sew. The boys couldn't go. They had their chores.

Finally it was suggested that one of the youngest children should go, but Uncle Otto shook his head.

"No," he said. "That's foolish. The child would not benefit from the journey, and she would be a burden for Amanda."

Uncle Otto looked around the table at the children. All nine of them. They all straightened up in their chairs and waited breathlessly.

"I think," Uncle Otto walked over to the stove to knock the ashes from his pipe, "I think the middle child should go." —

Then we children would ask Mother breathlessly, "And you were the middle one?"

Each time she would answer modestly,

"I was the middle one. I was the one chosen to go to Sweden with my mother when I was twelve years old."

We would sit and wonder what it must have been like to have been chosen to go to Sweden when you were twelve years old.

Mother's friendship with Nancy has endured over fifty years through letters and pictures. Only once in these many years have the two friends met.

And so it was with some emotion that we pulled into the

farmyard and looked at the comfortable old farm house standing alone on the Kansas plain and wondered what Nancy would be like. Mother hadn't seen her in forty years. I only in my imagination. For a moment, I wanted to run away. She was such a delightful person in my mind. Perhaps seeing the real Nancy would be a great disappointment.

Just then Nancy came to the back door. And it truly was Nancy, the skipping and singing Nancy my mother met in 1904. It was not the twelve-year-old Nancy. O no, she was a grandmother with lines on her face, but the skipping and singing heart was still there.

We sat in the cozy kitchen and enjoyed freshly baked oatmeal cookies and coffee with thick cream and we talked and laughed and cried together as good friends ought to do. On the table next to a pot of the largest and brightest African violets I've ever seen, was a worn Bible and a pair of spectacles.

We couldn't stay long. There were many people and other places to go on this trip, but as long as I live I shall be glad that we stopped to see Nancy. It does something for my soul to see this stamp of beauty on the faces of those who walk humbly with God on the plains of Kansas or wherever God puts them. Nancy's life might seem limiting to some, but it is as wide as eternity and as deep.

Spiritual Exercise: Write one letter to a friend you haven't seen in a long time. Don't chronicle your busyness, your troubles, your successes. Instead mention how, when you were eating your mother's homemade tarts last night, you remembered that Christmas you were snowed in at the dorm, and the only package to get through was a box of these tarts, or that you heard Verdi's "Requiem Mass" last night and it made you think of that wonderful year in Philadelphia, or .... Include the person you write to in your letter to him or her.

Old friends are not necessarily the best friends, but they can be good friends if we don't treat them as if they were bill collectors or census takers.

Ponder Romans 12:10, Romans 14:7, Hebrews 13:1, I Peter 1:22, and I Peter 1:24,25.

21

WHO HASN'T KNOWN SADNESS?

Small Talk: Over the radio the other night an announcer spoke of the book, *Bonjour Tristesse*. As an after-thought he said, "Wonder what that means?"

I am not fluent in French, but I learned a word or two during the three years I spent in Switzerland. I suppose it simply means a greeting or salute to sadness or melancholy. The book is about a sad time in a woman's life; thus the author entitled it, "Hello, Sadness."

The mood of people today is sadness, a prominent philosopher observed a few years ago. Now that I have reported this sad observation, I am not certain what I want to say about it.

I jotted it down in a book alongside a verse from Psalm 139. That was three years ago, and so for the third time on the twenty-seventh of September this message has greeted me, "The mood of people today is sadness."

Perhaps by passing it on to you, I can remove it from my mind.

I'm afraid not.

I find myself repeatedly asking,

"Is the mood of people today sadness?"

While walking on the Near North Side of Chicago in the later afternoon the other day, I passed a woman with untidy, streaked hair, wearing a dirty black dress. She was rummaging in a trash can. Within minutes I was stepping aside to let another lady, stunningly dressed, enter a long black car awaiting her in front of the all-glass apartment building on Lake Shore Drive.

The only thing these women had in common was what the philosopher was talking about, sadness. They both were sad. At least they appeared sad to me, and as far as that goes, maybe I seemed sad to them, too, but interestingly enough neither of these sad women saw me.

The one was intent on the possible treasures in the trash can, and the other was absorbed in her hair-do. A gust of wind from the lake was threatening a blue-silver strand from the pompadour. Therein might be a clue to sadness, not all sadness, but much sadness. Sad people see only themselves. They are forever bumping into mirrors.

Now that the philosopher has made me think about this, I am forced to agree with him. People are sad. But here the sage and I part company, not only in this age. People in any age are sad when they see not the Saviour.

The verse next to this scribbled thought about sadness in my devotional book is this one: "When I awake, I am still with thee." I have never yet read that beautiful, bright sentence without its causing a smile to break on my gloomy face. In fact, the entire 139th Psalm splinters soul-darkness the way lightning cracks the blackened sky in a harsh summer storm. It begins with God and ends with God, and yet it is all about you and me. "O Lord, Thou hast searched me . . . O Lord, try me . . . O Lord, lead me . . . ."

Lead me in the way everlasting.

Who hasn't known sadness? Who hasn't greeted the dawn with a heaviness of spirit? Who hasn't known utter defeat? Who hasn't failed himself so thoroughly that he wished he could crawl in a hole and die? Who hasn't experienced the agony of misunderstanding? Who hasn't tasted some bitterness?

It is in times like these that only God knows the avenue to the heart. "When I awake, I am still with thee." Yes, Lord, lead me in the way everlasting.

Spiritual Exercise: Read Psalm 139.

Small Prayer: Remind me, God, that this is a right glorious age I live in, as glorious as that of the downcast Abraham Lincoln when an entire nation dreaded each dawn. Help me to catch hold of the truth that any age can be transformed into glory as long as there is one man left to cry out, "With Thy help, O my God, I shall do what I can to overcome evil with good, sadness with joy, tears with laughter."

22

IT'S BETTER AHEAD

Small Talk: So you are seventy today, possibly eighty. I have a friend in Minneapolis who is ninety-seven. She is failing a little, true. She used to put four lumps of sugar in her coffee, now she only uses three. Her new doctor cut her down to three. My friend has outlived several doctors. "I have respected each one of my doctors," she said solemnly, "but I don't believe in doing everything they tell me." And in went the fourth lump of sugar.

I wonder what she would have thought of a health column I read last night in the newspaper. "Whether we like it or not," droned this doctor, "most of us will die in our seventy's and eighty's and will have to endure some senility for five years, ten years or longer before our final breath is drawn."

She probably would have snorted and gone on with her sewing, her reminiscing, her praying, her hoping, and her living.

Then there is Grandma Amole in Pennsylvania. We recently started corresponding. I was gone from my home for ten days this summer, and when I came back to my mail, there were three letters and two post cards from her. For an 87-year-old lady she is "drawing that final breath" with some vigor. I can barely squeeze a letter a year out of some of my younger, hardier friends.

There was one point in the health column with which I am in total agreement. The doctor said, "The future belongs to those who prepare for it. The time to prepare for your seventy's and eighty's is really in your thirty's and forty's." True, true, but then he had to add this chiller: "One must gather the harvest before the first blast of winter."

Gather the harvest! Many of us youngsters in our thirty's and forty's feel as if we've hardly begun to sow. This wierd philosophy of "button up your thin overcoat for the long, cruel winter ahead" does nothing to cause me to live cheerfully today, let alone hopefully on to the "final gasp."

I read to my mother the part about having to endure some senility before the final breath is drawn. After all, she is close to seventy. This "enduring senility" should be right down her alley. Only trouble, I couldn't sit her down long enough to observe how she is enduring it.

She was meeting "the girls" from her confirmation class for lunch, but first there was the bandage group down at church. Then she was putting some pies in the oven, because some relatives were coming for supper.

About ten that night we were seated quietly in the Grandma Room. I thought, now aha, I'll get proof that growing older is dismal. She interrupted my thought, "Have you seen the satellite? Last night about 11, Dave called. I had just gone to bed. He said, 'Mother, have you seen the satellite?' I slipped on my robe and went out in the backyard and looked straight up. I could see it so plain. It was a little larger than a star and moving fast. Isn't it wonderful?"

Think I'll go to bed now.

I want to get rested up for the years ahead.

Something tells me it gets better as you go along, and I don't want to miss any of the enchantment of growing older by being tired and worn out.

Spiritual Exercise: Read Psalm 150.

PART 5

Thankfully

23

NEVER DIE OF ORDINARINESS

Small Talk: A friend in Duluth spent a year in a convent. One of her favorite teachers was an Irish nun. Sister Brigetta repeatedly admonished her young charges — rolling her "r's" — "Girls, don't ever die of ordinariness."

I was with two women last night who shall never die of ordinariness. They are a mother-daughter writing team. Someone asked, "Do you always agree?"

The daughter smiled, "Seldom."

"We argue in a friendly way," the mother added.

These two ladies have been writing articles for more than fifteen years, ever since the mother came to live with her daughter. She explained, "I could quickly see that I would turn into a whining old lady if I didn't have something definite to do. I love to be busy."

She gave her daughter an affectionate look and continued, "Mary took care of the home and cooking so efficiently there was nothing I could add there. I wasn't handy with a needle, and I had no hobbies, other than reading; so I started going to the neighborhood library every day

"At lunch one day I told Mary about a man I had been reading about who trains wild animals without cages or fences. She looked at me and said, 'Mother, that would make a good article. Why don't you write it up?'

"Me, write an article? Why, I have no idea.

"The next morning I found an article in a newspaper about my interesting man and I started jotting down notes. That night I read them to Mary. 'Not bad,' she said, 'but it's pretty much of a jumble. Let me try to outline it or something.'"

And from that time on, this mother who did not want to turn into a whining old lady, and her daughter who had majored in chemistry, started writing articles — articles about everything and anything that interested them. They have worked hard, but as the daughter said, "We've had a peck of fun too," and best of all, the grandmother has turned into a winning, young person, a delight to all those who meet her, simply because she refused to die of ordinariness.

It is easy to die of ordinariness. In fact, very easy. We need only look around to see how many are. It takes fiery determination to put a halt to one's complaints and look the day squarely in the eye and begin to examine what small thing can be done this very day to take one brave step away from ordinariness.

Any of us can spend the rest of our life wishing things were different. This is the surest way to die of ordinariness. Things are as they are. We are as we are. What one little thing, then, can I do today to move out of the sphere of ordinariness? What can you do?

We can be kind one to another. This is a far nobler thing than many of us suspect. It is impossible for a man to live a good, pure and gentle life without the world being better for it; and the evidence of this goodness, purity and gentleness is expressed in small acts of kindness which we can do right today.

I believe that the starting point for extraordinary living is in this prayer. "Lord, Thou hast given me so very much, give me one thing more, a thankful heart."

I have yet to meet a person with a truly thankful heart toward God and his fellow man who is not living an extraordinary life.

There is another thing in this quest not to die of ordinariness. It has much to do with being one's self. It is your discovering who you are and then being you to the fullest extent, and I making the same discovery about myself.

One afternoon a few weeks ago I was listening to the Classical Music Hour on my FM radio. Actually I was half-listening, because I was reading at the same time. I really do not approve of this, listening to good music and reading simultaneously, but nevertheless, I was doing it. I was paying enough attention to the music to hear it announced that the next selection was to be "Hark, Hark, the Lark."

I didn't pay too much attention to it, but it did register with me that it got off to a peculiar start, for a lark, that is; but my book suddenly became very interesting and I forgot I was listening to "Hark, Hark, the Lark."

Suddenly I put down the book and concentrated with my full faculties on the music. I realized that all the time I had been reading I had been most unhappy about this lark. Something had been registering in my subconscious mind that this was a frightfully disturbed bird. The sounds coming from the radio were dissonant and quite unlarklike, another victim of the turbulent twentieth century.

Believe me, it was a real relief when the announcer said at the end of the number, "I beg your pardon, we are *now* going to play 'Hark, Hark, the Lark.' The selection you have just heard was . . . . by . . . ." Both names unpronounceable and unrememberable. It was not the sort of music I enjoy. Neither is "Hark, Hark, the Lark" one of my favorites, but it did sound good when the gentle music came into the room, because it was true to itself.

There is a big lesson in this story. Be yourself. With all that is in you, be you. Don't be someone else. Be you. Did it ever occur to you that there is no one else in the whole wide world quite like you?

Few people are being themselves today. It seems everyone wants to be somebody else. This is silly. You are you. I am I. For better or for worse. When we try to be other than the persons God created, we don't ring true.

I *knew* that wasn't "Hark, Hark, the Lark."

It couldn't be.

And thank goodness it wasn't.

I heard Anna Rose Wright, the author of several delightful children's books, speak last week. I have never met anyone who was more genuinely herself than this amiable writer. It was one of the most refreshing experiences to listen to someone who wasn't trying to impress anyone, but was simply being herself, and we could take her or leave her, and nearly everyone in the audience took her and took her right into their hearts. Don't die of ordinariness; be yourself. Thank God for your life and live it to His pleasing.

Spiritual Exercise: Walk to the library and pick out a biography or an autobiography of some happy, extraordinary person. Here are a few suggestions, people well worth reading about: John Wesley, Oswald Chambers, Hannah W. Smith, Jenny Lind, Martin Luther, Thomas Kelly, Max Beerboom, George F. Handel, Eugenia Price, Ole Bull, Henry Drummond, and many, many more. I am not evaluating these people; I am merely saying there seems to be a relationship between their extraordinariness, their thankfulness and their joy.

24

DIFFICULT BUT NOT IMPOSSIBLE

Small Talk: David Garrick, the famous English actor, was showing Samuel Johnson through his vast estate and mansion. After the lengthy, exhausting tour, Johnson shook his head and said, "Ah, David, David, these are the things that make the deathbed terrible!"

The historicity of that scene I question. It is a little too neat to sound true; but the anecdote underlines a tremendous truth. The more you have in material possessions, the harder it is to let go — even unto death. But at the same time, we need to clear up one common misconception.

There is a "sort" of religious person who revels in picking on the man with wealth almost as if this rich man is a tintype of the anti-Christ. One would assume their Bibles read, "It is impossible for a rich man to enter heaven." But no, the Holy Scripture does not say that. "It will be *hard*," Christ said, "for a rich man to enter heaven."

It will be difficult, yes, or hard, whatever word you like; but the Lord did not say, "impossible." Hard and impossible are miles apart. Possessions will never keep a man out of heaven. It is what he does with his possessions and his attitude toward his wealth that can make life and death either dreadful or wonderful.

To those who have been given more, there is always that joyous possibility of giving away more, joyous for both the donor and the receiver. The person who has a lot and keeps it misses the whole point of why he has so much; no wonder his life generally has a tragic ending.

I remember an incident in Sweden a few years ago which helped me to see how even a few "possessions" can alter one's attitude. Some friends and I were scheduled to take a boat from our hotel on Lake Siljan to the town of Mora. Our luggage was piled on the pier, and we were ready to go.

To the surprise of all, the small steamer sailed past the dock without even a friendly toot of the whistle. We waved and shouted. The hotel manager jumped up and down, but the captain definitely was not including the Persborg guests in that day's outing. It was the weekend of Midsummer's Day, Sweden's most important holiday, so things were not normal.

The hotel manager started throwing our luggage back into the trunk of his car. He was still sputtering about the boat not stopping, so we didn't ask, but we got the idea he was going to drive us to Mora.

We roared up the hill to the main road. As he was still scowling and muttering (he had better things to do on Midsummer's Day than to drive forty miles to Mora and back), I thought it best not to mention to him that he had failed to shut the trunk. As we raced over the gravel road, in and out of birch trees, it was one of the most anxious rides of my life.

Once we were delivered to the Mora station, and all luggage miraculously still intact, we sat and laughed about the ride. My friends were particularly amused, because it was the first time they had seen me visibly upset on the trip. We had been on far rougher rides than this short trip to Mora, and I had taken each of these emergencies with a serenity which can only be described as maddening to all those in the same situation who are not reacting calmly.

It was easy for me to be unruffled in Rome when our luggage didn't turn up where it was supposed to and we had to sit in the dismal customs room for two hours while worried officials ran here and there trying to find our suitcases, or the time we had to throw the luggage out the window at Aigle, because the Milano Express only stops one minute at this village in the Rhone Valley, because all of my possessions could easily have been replaced. I have traveled long enough to know I should bring only my oldest clothes and few of them on a long trip. It is easy to be casual about losing things or having them slung out the window when you have nothing to lose. But in Sweden I bought some gifts, dishes, an Orrefors vase, and a painting or two; and suddenly I did care violently whether or not my luggage bounced out of an open trunk.

David Garrick's problem was not that he had too much, but that he was too enmeshed in his possessions to cheerfully accept the invitation to leave them behind someday. That is one of the reasons it is difficult for a rich man to enter heaven; not because it is evil to be wealthy, no, but because it is so hard to leave it all behind.

A person has to work out a way of living which involves sharing, because it is the only way he can leave this earth willingly. Indeed it must be heartbreaking to look upon one's vast estate and suddenly realize that it all has to be left behind someday.

But the wise man and the thankful man who has shared his good things can go home softly and gently, because he has the hidden treasures of life in his heart, and these he may take with him.

Spiritual Exercise: Give something away this day that you know you can't take with you.

25

"ONE MAN CANNOT UNTIE HIMSELF"

Small Talk: Success never comes overnight. Neither do happiness, poise, contentment, well being, or any of those nice sounding words. They might seem to, but they never do. Nor are they fixed entities that once we have brushed, we can hold. They come and go. Come and go. And the longer I live, the more clearly I am seeing how much of my contentment, happiness, minor successes, very minor, have been set into motion toward me by other people, by my best friends.

A prominent businessman was telling about his early years. "I didn't have any confidence," he said, "hardly a shred. Shortly after I got my job, another young man came into our office. Herb had a pleasant, happy personality. We soon became good friends.

"I didn't catch on until years after, but nearly every time Herb and I got together, he had something good to tell me, something that he seemed to sense would give me a lift. If he had heard one of the office girls say that I was the best dressed fellow in the office, he would report this back to me.

"I can remember one day he told me that the boss had said that he wished he had more hard workers like me. I can't tell you what those remarks did for me."

He paused, then added, "Herb had a lot to do with getting me going. I really didn't know I was appreciated in that office, but with my friend continually telling me I was, I guess I just worked the harder. But it was deeper than that. Herb believed in me, and I guess I just sort of hated to let him down!"

That is pretty sound advice, this passing on nice things you hear. For fun I tried it the other day. It went farther than I expected. This is the way it came about: Recently I introduced a young minister's wife (a busy woman with four small children, a part-time job, her house and husband to take care of, plus many church duties) to a friend of mine who is an artist.

Later the artist friend told me she was very impressed with the young mother, and that she thought she would make a lovely subject for a portrait. "She has a beautiful face," she concluded.

The next time I saw "the little mother" I passed on this information. It happened to be Monday morning, and Monday's washday, you know, even in the manse. I didn't let the fact that she was standing knee-deep in dirty clothes in the basement dressed in a faded housecoat with curlers in her hair and not a suggestion of make-up on deter me from giving every last shining detail down to the fact that the artist had said that she would make a lovely subject for a portrait.

She gave me a wild look, but didn't say anything. It is impossible to talk above that machine. She shouted to me to go on upstairs and put on the coffee.

When she finally came up, she sat at the table and was absentmindedly taking out the curlers. "Thanks," she said, when I poured the coffee. We're good friends, or I wouldn't have stopped on a Monday morning, you understand. Her voice sounded far away, "Did she really say I had a beautiful face?"

I nodded and helped myself to another sweet roll. Just then three of the four children bounded in, and so that was the end of the conversation.

I forgot all about it until I appeared at the door again in a couple of weeks, and it was a Monday again. The moment she opened the door I could sense something.

"Isn't this washday?" I asked.

"Yes, it is," she smiled.

"But you're kind of dressed up or something?"

She nodded, "I decided after our talk the other day that if the Lord has given me a little comeliness, I should have the decency to share it with my family and friends, too!"

This time I had had the decency to call a few hours before I arrived to say that I was dropping by later in the day.

Both of us learned from this experience more than we expected. It seemed to open up to each of us our responsibility to one another. There is an African proverb: "One man cannot untie himself." It helps untie a person to know others think good thoughts about him, or think about him at all. I have only one friend who does not respond to this law of life as Paul stated it in Philippians, "Let each of you esteem and look upon and be concerned for not (merely) his own interests, but also each for the interests of others." This "friend" rarely acknowledges letters and the other small things that friends say, do, and send. She is totally unapproachable, because she interprets every move toward her as a sign of weakness, as an invasion of her privacy. Believe me, I have been very tempted to simply let go. So this friend no longer wants my friendship, tiddlely pom; so what, there are other people, don't waste emotion on one ungrateful person; but it is not that easy.

If I let go of this friend, I would have to let go of something I believe in with all my heart and soul, loyalty. This quality is not too well known in our age. People make vows and break them with scarcely a yawn in between. We used to be concerned when we heard of a divorce. Today we barely raise an eyebrow when we read of some one marrying for the third or fourth time. I heard a minister say once, "At least we Americans are not like the French who openly live in adultery." I'm not too sure God looks with favor on any person who treats vows lightly.

When I enter into friendship with others, I don't make any official declaration, to be sure, but something registers inside me that this is a forever thing. It is absolutely impossible for me to be indifferent to a friend. I am not in any way trying to give you a picture of me as a glorified knight from King Arthur's Round Table whose motives are purity themselves. Not at all. Believe me, my friends have to put up with an awful lot, and as it is true in all human relationships, I have to put up with their weaknesses and faults; but here is the heart of real friendship. Two friends are people who care for one another more "in spite of" than "because of."

I shall go on waiting for my friend. Some day she'll come to see that I need her, and the small joke of the matter, she needs me. It is not an un-Christian characteristic to need friends. For me one of the loveliest pictures of Jesus is to see Him walking with His friends. If the Son of God needed friends, surely I need not apologize for my need. I need only say, "Thank You, Lord, for the wonderful people You have given to be my friends."

Shakespeare was very mindful of the truth that our emotional stability to a large degree depends on others. Several of his masterful plays dwell on this theme. The longer I ponder this, the more it sweeps over me, my responsibility to others.

Shortly after Christmas I got awfully busy. I am not one to like busy-ness. I really wasn't made for this age, and so to remove a little pressure, I wrote to my sister in Texas and told her not to expect to hear from me for the next month or two, that I was working on a very "important project." While I was writing the letter, the phone rang. A friend's voice came over the wire, "I'm not going to take your time, but I just wanted to tell you something. I sent one of your columns to an old aunt of mine who lives in a nursing home. I just got a postcard from her. This is what she wrote, 'That article you sent was like a drink of cool water from our well back on the farm.' 'Bye. See you Thursday night.'"

I walked back to the desk. Very slowly. I sat hunched over with my chin supported in my hands, and I simply sat there for several minutes. Then I picked up the letter I had just written, crumpled it fiercely, and pitched it in the basket at my feet, picked up my pen and wrote a cheerful postcard to the dear ones in Texas.

Who am I to think that my time is more valuable than their time? If my sister is willing to take precious moments from her busy schedule as a mother and minister's wife to write to me, I surely have time to write to them too, if I love them.

"One man cannot untie himself." Friends, husbands, wives, children: " . . . Be ye kind one to another, tenderhearted, forgiving one another, even as God for Christ's sake hath forgiven you."

> 'Twas a thief said the last
> kind word to Christ:
> Christ took the kindness
> and forgave the theft.
> —Robert Browning

I'd a thousand times rather be remembered as a kind person than a successful writer. We might be people nearly choked with faults, weaknesses, undesirable character traits, but there is not one of us who cannot reach toward this goal of extending a kind word here, a kind word there.

Spiritual Exercise: If you have heard anything nice about a person, be sure to pass on the information. If you have heard anything unkind, wrap it up and take it home with you. It will make marvelous material for prayer.

PART 6

Simply But Deeply

*He hath shewed thee, O man, what
is good; and what doth the Lord require of thee, but to do justly, and to
love mercy, and to walk humbly with
thy God.* —Micah 6:8

26

GLORIOUS SILENCE

Small Talk: A number of rousing messages and sermons have
been given on the subject of life after death. Gradually it has
been catching up with me, that many of these stirring, trium-
phant, boisterous words go over my head.

I prefer to contemplate death, and what lies beyond it,
quietly. My capacity to absorb the noisy words of men is shrink-
ing, and mercifully, I find that I am about at the end of my
loud talking.

In these discordant days I care only to listen to the words
of the Galilean. He offers the only Easter message that holds me,
that will quiet me in that hour when in the midst of my unfin-
ished projects, a shadow will fall across my life and I'll look up
in surprise, "O Death! I was not looking for you so soon."

What would happen, one Easter, if the churches around the
world kept silent? No message. No lessons. Choirs quiet. Or-
ganists, trumpeters, and violinists sitting with folded hands. No
collection. No children reciting poems. Silence. Only silence.
Glorious silence. And in the silence believers wondering about
the Man, Jesus, who noiselessly came out of a tomb.

Glorious silence. Only silence. Silence to ponder His Easter
message, "Let not your hearts be troubled."

It is a relief to me to learn that all God asks of me is to
believe in Him and the One He sent. "Let not your heart be
troubled: ye believe in God, believe also in me." Beautifully
simple words, and aren't they simply beautiful?

No longer do I have to ponder whether this denomination or that one has "the truth." I need not know Hebrew and Greek to understand the words of Christ, nor do I have to concern myself whether the streets of heaven are solid gold or if this is beautiful imagery attempting to express the timelessness of eternity. I don't have to bog down myself because there seems to be so little real understanding among men. And happily, I do not have to ponder where heaven is, and what we're going to do in the land of forever and forever, nor need I put my peanut brain to work on what forever is!

No, I thank my God that He only asks me to believe Him, and this I do, quietly and in awe, as a child. I worked at being a "spiritual giant" for a short spell, but found it didn't become me at all. I became so heavy. It even hurt to laugh, because this strained some muscles. I am quite content these days simply to be a child of the Heavenly Father and let Him proportion out for me what light, what joy, what grievance I need for the day.

There is a lovely French song called "The Three Bells." In the first verse we hear about the birth of Jean Francois, and as the village church bells ring out in the chorus, they joyfully herald the birth of this child. We learn in the second verse that Jean Francois has grown to young manhood, and this time the bells ring out because it is the day of his wedding. When the bells toll for the third and last time, we know that Jean Francois is dead.

It is when the bells ring the third time for each of us that we need words that are neither lofty nor loud. That is when the quiet and real words of the Saviour hold a man as no other words can. "Let not your heart be troubled," He whispers to every troubled heart. "Ye believe in God, believe also in me. In my Father's house are many mansions: if it were not so, I would have told you. I go to prepare a place for you. And if I go and prepare a place for you, I will come again, and receive you unto myself; that where I am, there ye may be also."

That is good enough for me to know that where He is, I will be someday. O, surely He has risen!

I believe in God and His only Son and to know Him is life everlasting. O World, be still and listen to the Galilean in these troubled days. He ever speaks to the listening heart, and His words are simply beautiful.

Spiritual Exercise: Read Psalm 46 followed by silent prayer.

27

"I DON'T NEED ANYTHING"

Small Talk: A friend a few years ago told me, "Don't preach at people; don't take it upon yourself to reform, instruct and tell people what is wrong with them. There are heaps of preachers and teachers and others who can do this and are doing it. Simply give your readers the love of God in the measure in which His love spills over into your heart."

It is a good thing I found that note, because I was just getting wound up to give a preaching, expounding, and instructing treatise on the book of Romans. In fact, I had prepared some "tremendous" notes to hurl at my readers, but I am quietly putting them away until I have digested them myself more thoroughly. May I suggest though, read the book of Romans. That is what I have been doing recently, and it is a little like taking spiritual vitamin tablets. Paul's faith was so vital, so dynamic, so on fire, it does not harm a man to try to analyze what made him that way.

I was having a "man-to-man" talk with a small nephew the other day, and we were talking about the Bible. I had just remarked that the Bible was all about Jesus. And he nodded and said, "Yes, it's all about the cross of Jesus."

When I talk with this five-year-old lad, I feel somewhat like Plato addressing Socrates. I love children, particularly when they are dead serious. And this they can be. As Charlie seemed to be in an instructing mood, I asked him what was his favorite Bible verse. He pursed his lips and frowned deeply as if his little mind was sweeping the entire Word of God to fasten on to this one verse. Finally, and in this dead-serious way, he said, "As a matter of fact, it's that one — O, *you* know! The Lord is my Shepherd, I don't need anything."

Well, I didn't know exactly that one, but the more I've thought about it, the more I like Charlie's version.

"I don't need anything" sounds more positive than "I shall not want," and if there is one needful thing among us Christians today, it is to be more positive.

Most of us respond to this positive element in individuals. From Paul to our present generation, the ones who have encouraged us in our faith are the ones who have trusted God with everything that was in them.

God honors this trust, not by giving these undaunted believers a little white cottage with roses and a pension at the end of life's trail — not at all. Sometimes these great trusters of God don't even have two-room apartments to finish out their days, but He gives them something else, something infinitely more dear than material security. He gives them Himself.

I am glad chapter nine follows chapter eight in Romans. Here we see the dynamic, soaring Paul as a broken-hearted man. It hardly sounds at all like the same man who just a few words before was flying higher than an eagle. But this is a true slice of life. Life is laden with contrast. Life is contrast. We're up. We're down. We have fleeting moments of being "more than conquerors," and then we fall on our faces and cry, "Nobody knows the trouble I've seen."

But one reason I keep going back to Romans, Paul helps to remind me never to lose track of one great hope. God is in it all, and nothing, nothing, nothing shall ever separate you or me from the love of God in Christ Jesus.

Spiritual Exercise: Study Romans 8:14-39 and Romans 9:1-5.

28

THINK THE BEST

Small Talk: As Mark Twain said, "Few of us can stand prosperity. Another man's, I mean." If there is one secret (but I know there isn't) why some people are happier than others, it is tied up with how and what they think of others, particularly their friends.

If a good friend of yours has written a best seller (and you are an unsuccessful writer) and on an upper shelf in your mind rests this thought, "Isn't that wonderful? I'm so happy for him," then you, my friend, are a happy person, and may I add, a rare person, a person who has entered deep into the heart of Christ.

Perhaps I can illustrate it this way.

Let's say you move to a city where you formerly lived. You send out notes to old friends giving the approximate date of your arrival. The day you move in there is a letter from one neighbor welcoming you back home. Within a few days all the friends acknowledge in one way or another that they are glad you are back among them. All except one, the friend who has written the best seller.

You are most understanding the first few days and weeks. After all, he is a busy person, an important person with many responsibilities. You must be willing to give him more time.

A few more days go by. Your thinking shifts a little. He is probably out of town or he did not get your note. By accident you learn he is in town, he did get the note, and out stalks the three-headed monster: doubt, envy, and fear. "The Thing" sits and stares at you, nodding in agreement with a thought forming in your mind.

For the first time you begin to doubt this friend. The head with the sassy green eyes smirks, "Nice loyal guy, your pal, sure eager to see his old friend."

Then fear thrusts out his unsightly head and sneers, "What makes you think you have anything to offer this friendship? You're strictly the minor league, and . . . ."

The heads keep interrupting one another, and they pommel you far into the night. Suddenly you remember Martin Luther and his ink pot. You reach for the nearest heavy object to hurl at the adversary. It's your Bible.

All three heads watch in morbid fascination.

"You wouldn't throw *that*?" they say in unison.

"No, I don't need to throw it, I only need to read it. Listen." You read from one of the Psalms, "Wait on the Lord: be of good courage, and he shall strengthen thine heart: wait, I say, on the Lord." When you look up from the page the unwelcome visitor is gone.

The friend still does not call or write, but now you are able to wait in a different spirit, a spirit of restful trusting. You make a point, though, to pray every day that God will call to your remembrance only good and kind thoughts about the friend, and even more than this, that you might think the highest and best toward this person who is causing you some discomfort at the moment.

I am not trying to say that this is some magic cure-all for all strained relationships. Not at all. In fact, there are no perfect relationships in life. We should count it great gain if we have one or two friends who seem to understand. We all fail one another from time to time, but I have never seen a person harmed by my thinking and hoping the highest and best for him; and I have even had the delight in seeing myself reach higher because someone gave me credit for being better than I am.

None of us is immune to some envy, fear and doubt. No not one. But that doesn't mean we need to listen every day to the three-headed monster.

When I lived in Minnesota not too long ago, I remember reading about a young man who at the age of 38 became the president of a bank. A friend commented, "I want you to watch this fellow. Up until this promotion he is well liked in this community, and there is 'no fault in him.' But you wait. He'll get it in a short while."

In a few months he was made a deacon in his church, and sure enough, within days we heard such talk, "So now he has to be a big wheel in church too — not content to just be the top boy at the bank."

My good friend remarked philosophically, "I believe in thinking the best of people. Maybe the banker goes to church for the same reason we do, to learn more about a Saviour who helps free men from fear, envy and doubt."

Spiritual Exercise for the day: Read Mark 10:42-45; Proverbs 22:4, 10, 11; Romans 12:3, 9, 10, 21.

29

COME SAIL WITH ME

Small Talk: There is nothing like an ocean voyage, so they say. I'm sure you are familiar with this picture: A handsome ship gliding through blue, still waters, and a couple in fashionably casual clothes playing shuffleboard on deck with a warm sun smiling down on them.

May I share with you a few of my ocean experiences? There was that time on the Swiss freighter when we ran into a freak storm on the "usually" placid green Mediterranean. The only thing green in a few minutes was our faces. We didn't have time to "secure" anything but ourselves, and this we did by hurtling ourselves into our respective bunks. All night long our eleven suitcases, the chairs and waste basket shuffled back and forth across our stateroom (a shuffleboard of a different variety than that advertised in the alluring travel folders) and every muscle in our bodies ached from holding on in our bunks to keep from joining the pitching gear.

Or that trip I took from Hawaii to San Francisco. I remember remarking as we were gliding out of the harbor in Honolulu, "You hardly know the ship is moving." Then we hit the open sea, and I hit my bunk. Several others in our group who also were seasick would mournfully whisper every once in awhile when they could find the strength, "You hardly know the ship is moving!" Finally they dragged some of us out on an open deck the third day to see if the icy air could do anything for us. By this time, my friends weren't able to even taunt me with, "You hardly know the ship is moving." All the bracing air did for me was convince me that traveling by air was the only way.

I am beginning to suspect that smooth ocean cruises exist only in novels and on travel folders, but I'm still hopeful and I keep trying.

A few years ago I went to Europe on the *Ile de France,* supposedly one of the steadiest ships of its day. It was wonderfully steady, that is, until she hit hurricane "Jane." From that time on, fortunately, I don't remember a thing about the trip. A doctor friend of mine was experimenting with a new type of seasick medicine. His remedy was so effective I slept through nearly the entire trip.

So next I tried the *Queen Elizabeth* (it is hard for me to give up). I had an almost written statement that the *Queen Elizabeth* always has a smooth crossing. And so, did we have a smooth trip? Did we enjoy shuffleboard on deck? Was the sun warm and soothing? This trip was so rough they had to use the stabilizers.

This was something new to me. On the last day out, I was able to lift my head slightly and converse with the steward when he brought me my crackers and green pills. He told me that these stabilizers cost a couple million dollars, but we both agreed it was well worth it. They eliminate sideward rolling.

Stabilizers are something like big fins which come out on either side of the ship and they help to balance it. I have no idea how they work, but they do work. Another ship plowing through similar waters would have pitched all over; but the stabilizers did keep the ship from rolling.

A Christian is somewhat like a ship with stabilizers. He isn't spared from high seas. His life is often right in the midst of swirl; but with his stabilizers of faith, he can be held steady even though he goes through turbulent water.

An interesting side feature about the *Queen Elizabeth* stabilizers, and I'm quoting the steward, "The stabilizers are absolutely ineffective when the waves come head on. They can't act then. They would snap off. Those waves exert a tremendous pressure."

"That's when sailing is rugged, eh?"

He grinned, "That's right. That's when you wish you had followed your father's advice and gone into the shoe business with him."

This pattern is true in life too. When we deliberately defy

God and head into trouble, our stabilizers of faith won't work —
that is, until we get right with God again.

Spiritual Exercise: If there is any area in your lives where you
are deliberately and persistently disobeying God, dare pray this
prayer: "Search me, O God, and know my heart: try me, and
know my thoughts: and see if there be any wicked way in me,
and lead me in the way everlasting."

30

A GOD WHO REVEALS SECRETS

Small Talk: A writer forever seeks to say something that will
cause his reader to inwardly exclaim, "I know this feeling," or to
say, "That happened to me once." If he can do this, he will
write words that span centuries. I'm thinking of an incident in
history that Daniel recorded. "And in the second year of the
reign of Nebuchadnezzar," Daniel wrote, "Nebuchadnezzar
dreamed dreams, wherewith his spirit was troubled, and his
sleep brake from him."

I for one can surely say, "I know this feeling." Can't you?
Whenever I do have a sleepless night, I generally spend the
time thanking God that I don't have them very often. It is one
of the more lonely things common to man to lie awake at night
and hear the clock strike two or was that three? But you're not
that aroused to care to get up and see, so you just lie there and
listen to an occasional car go by or a far-away train whistle or,
if you are in a large city, the sirens.

To go on with Nebuchadnezzar. He didn't seem to like a
sleepless night either. He called for the wisest men in his country to interpret his troubling dream. They came, the magicians,
the astrologers, the sorcerers, and gathered around him. Just as
Nebuchadnezzar started to tell them his dream, he couldn't
remember it.

"The thing is gone from me," he exclaims.

That is a maddening feeling. It happened to me just the other morning. I started to tell a vivid dream I had had, and suddenly the thing was gone. Completely gone. We all laughed it off, and soon those of us at the breakfast table were talking about something else. But not so with Nebuchadnezzar and a young friend of mine.

Gary, when he was not quite three, started to say something to his mother, and then forgot what it was he was going to say. He was embarrassed and turned to her and asked her what it was he wanted to say. He was in tears before the session was over, because she simply did not know what he was thinking, and with the unreasonableness and credulity of a three-year-old, he insisted she should.

Nebuchadnezzar's wise men didn't do much better than Gary's mother. They flatly told the king,

"Sir, this is a rare thing that you require. There is not a man on earth who can do this."

But you did not talk that way to Nebuchadnezzar. He was furious and commanded that all the wise men of Babylon be slain.

It looked pretty hopeless for the wise men, but they weren't wise men for nothing. They figured there must be someone who could come up with an answer. "What about that intellectual, what's his name?" one of the magicians asked. "You know who I mean."

A light came into the eyes of the wisest sorcerer, "Daniel, Daniel, of course."

The wise men went to Daniel and begged him to save them. Daniel was one of the Jews who had been taken into captivity when Nebuchadnezzar besieged Jerusalem, and he already had gained a reputation for his great wisdom and understanding.

When Daniel saw the gravity of the suituation, he agreed to do what he could. The first thing he did, he went directly to the king to ask for time. It was granted to him. Next he went to his house and shared the problem before him with three loyal friends. Together the men prayed that God would reveal the secret of the king's dream to Daniel.

God answered the prayer. Then Daniel did a strange thing.

Instead of flying off to tell the king he had the dream, Daniel made another lengthy prayer. He thanked God for revealing the dream to him.

Then he went to the king.

Among the many wise things he told King Nebuchadnezzar, one particularly stands out to me. Daniel said, "There is a God in heaven who reveals secrets, King Nebuchadnezzar."

That is a jewel of great price to know and believe, to know and believe that God still is revealing secrets to those who trust Him. I believe one of God's secrets is in this story.

Daniel believed God. With this faith in a real God, he dared to ask the impossible. When God answered his prayer, Daniel first thanked God, then acted on the knowledge God gave him.

O we of little faith who listen to thousands of words every day spoken by fallible men, why do we cover our ears to the omnipotent, omniscient, holy God of time and eternity?

Last night when my sleep was broken from me, I read a couple of chapters in the book of Daniel. I cannot recall now what was troubling my spirit. The poetry and rhythm of Daniel's words crowded out the small worries, "There is a God in heaven that revealeth secrets."

Spiritual Exercise: Read Daniel, chapters 1 and 2.

PART 7

Truthfully

31

ONCE THERE WAS A SAD HOUSE

Small Talk: I like children. Not the fussy and bored and fearful and complaining tired ones. But children like my friend Chip. He was standing on the back porch one night when a storm slammed through his town. The earth quivered with each thunder clap and magnificent bolts of lightning split the darkened sky. Above the noise of the colliding clouds, this five-year-old shouted with glee, "God just took my picture!"

That's a wonderful God to have, one who cares so much for His children He takes a picture of them now and then. And what a flash bulb!

Then I rather like this young lad who told his mother and father he wasn't ready to go home from church because, said he, "I haven't seen God yet."

I am sure I'd like to know the child who wrote this "essay": "In the early morning, the air is fresher than further on in the day. You can smell pine trees, box hedges and flowers. When I go in, breakfast smells so good!"

I wonder if it is wrong to long for the air to smell fresher? I wonder if it is too late to become the people we meant to be? I wonder if only children have the right to love and hope and breathe deeply and live lives that skip along?

A seven-year-old child once asked her teacher, "How do people feel when they are grown up? Do they feel tall and fat? Do they feel all finished?"

That makes me shudder a little, because more than anything I want to escape crusting over, becoming tall, fat and finished; and yet it is no mystery to me to see how and why it happens to so many. It happens when we give up our dreams, our ideals, our singing, lofty pictures of what life ought to be. It happens when our friends fail us, when we fail them, when we no longer trust God, when we settle for less.

Often we draw around our shoulders the tall, fat and finished cloak when our plans do not work out just as we hoped. But can we not learn from David who was thwarted in his dream to build a great temple for God? God did not reveal to David why He said no to this seemingly good and noble thought of David. But David accepted God's no for the time being, and as he patiently waited for God, he used his energy and the time to gather the material which would be needed to build the temple when God was ready. As F. B. Meyer, that man of patience, said, "If you cannot have what you hoped, do not allow your energies to run to waste; but arise and help others to achieve. If you may not build, you may gather materials for him that shall."

What I am seeing along these lines I still have trouble getting into orderly words, but I know a small boy who almost said what I'm excited about. I don't believe he will mind if I share with you the story he wrote. The heading simply said, "Creative writing, Second Grade, Bloom School, Brad."

"Once there was a sad house. It was sad because it had no friends. One day some workers came and built a happy house right next to the sad house. The happy house always tried to make the sad house happy and gay. He tickled him, but he wouldn't even giggle. So he tried and tried and tried to be good. Pretty soon he was perfect. So he never was sad again."

Now everyone reading a story like that can come up with a different interpretation, and I've already had two or three, but this is the one that does the most for me.

Once there was a sad house. That could be you or me, or any of us entering this tall, fat, and finished stage. And the reason we are sad, Brad says, we have no friends. And so next in the story a real good thing happens. Some workers build a happy house right next to our sad house. And this happy house tried to make us happy. Oh, he tried, but nothing worked. The sad house was still sad. So sad.

Now the next three sentences come pretty fast; in fact, they sort of pile up on one another, and you slam right into the ending without too clear an idea what really did happen to make this story end so happily; because it does.

That "he tried and tried and tried" is the stage we're in. Actually it is life itself, this glorious, crazy mixture of sadness and happiness and defeat and joy and frustration and struggle. Which one of us doesn't try, try, try?

But what went on between the sad house trying and trying and trying and that amazing statement, "Pretty soon he was perfect," our young author was wise enough to leave alone. I like to think of that as God's place in the story. Then the story ends happily, "So he never was sad again."

Maybe this is one big difference between children and adults. Adults know they will be sad again.

But also we should keep our childlike hearts alive and remember there will be happy days again too. You need a young heart to keep joyously alert for the little, unexpected happy moments that skip across every day.

I have a friend whose husband divorced her awhile back. It was a blow, and I don't want you at all to get a picture of her grasping a positive thought or clutching a Bible verse and from then on being "radiantly happy." Life doesn't flow, it chugs; but the other night we were at a small party together, she went over to the hostess, a mutual friend of ours, and slipped her arm around her waist and said with simplicity, "This is such fun to be here." She'll make it all right, because she's living expectantly and is grateful for the friends she has who love her.

Spiritual Exercise: We really all need to war against becoming tall, fat, and finished. A good starting point is to ask God to make us more "simple." Just because everyone else in our block has a great big house and a great big yard and a great big car and a great big debt, do we need this? Maybe if we didn't spend so much of our time as janitors, gardeners, chauffers, keepers of museums and money borrowers, we'd be more like the young lad who wrote the essay, "When I go in, breakfast smells so good!" Remind us, dear God, that we are Thy children and that our steps and words should be light as Thou in love dost carry us forward. Help to unburden us from the "too much" in our lives.

32

SUCH LITTLE MEN

Small Talk: I overheard a woman say last night, "I'm no authority on art, but . . . ." She then proceeded to criticize with finality and wallop a whole ring-full of artists beginning with the first caveman who scratched a few strange marks on the wall of his cave down to our present colorful age. She ended her "art lecture" with a strong left jab at a local artist who had recently won a prize for an oil painting he had made of a cow and a barn. I gathered that it was one of these modern pieces where the viewer has difficulty ascertaining which blob is the cow and which is the barn.

I am not objecting to this lady having a strong, personal opinion and expressing it, but why didn't she come right out and say it without the embroidery, "I'm no authority on art, but . . ."?

Believe me, I am not picking only on this loud-voiced woman who is no authority on art. We all are guilty of pseudo-modesty, pretension and puffed-upness, some of the time, actually, too much of the time. If I had the nerve to peer back at the things I have written in the past few years, I probably would turn up several articles that began, "I'm no authority but . . . ."

Now that I've brought up this subject, we might as well go after it. I've noticed that one of the favorites in conversation is, "I don't know much, but . . . ." and then follows a barrel or a thimbleful of nectar from the speaker's storehouse of wisdom. I suppose one of the reasons we use this gimmick is that it is pleasantly humble sounding. It surely doesn't sound very good to come right out and say that you mean, "I know more about this subject than most people, and you better value my opinion" — that is, if we're at all interested in winning friends and keeping them, not to mention jobs, bonuses, chicken every Sunday, and two cars under the carport.

The woman whose remarks I overheard probably would resent my interpretation of her opening remark, but I honestly do not think I am too far off (and I mean this modestly; if someone can prove I'm wrong, I'll make a brave attempt to be gracious and admit my error). The thing that gave her away was the tone of her voice. Her words were hard, metallic, and clipped. Humility, the real thing, has a gentle sound, like Mozart as played by the Budapest quartet. This lady had a rock-and-roll delivery.

Haughtiness has a way of creeping into our speech if we indulge the habit of thinking too highly of ourselves, and not only our speech, but every area of our living; and if we are writers, speakers, ministers, heaven help us if we have little modesty and awareness of our limitations; we have a way of sounding more positive than we mean sometimes.

Is there anyone more unattractive than a puffed-up vicar, priest, or pastor? Or more deadly. And yet today we have among us far too many of these un-gentlemen. A young minister friend of mine was telling me about a recent meeting he had attended. "Here we were," he said, "hundreds of so-called men of God, and what did we do those three days we met together? Pray for our people, the nations, and ourselves? Oh no, we discussed pensions, higher salaries; we argued whether Mary was truly a virgin, what parts of the Bible are dubious; and we voted to unite with another church group whose love and respect for our historic faith is even colder than ours."

We are living in a day when it is popular to put God in His place. It is not at all uncommon to hear men stand in pulpits built by God-fearing, Bible-loving people and hear them make sport of those who in this "enlightened age" still hold fast to the Word of God. Actually there is nothing new about this. Paul had some clear and pointed words to say to the men of his generation who tried to match their wits with God. He put it this way, "The truth is that, although of course we lead normal human lives, the battle we are fighting is on the spiritual level ... Our battle is to bring down every deceptive fantasy and every imposing defense that men erect against the true knowledge of God. We even fight to capture every thought until it acknowledges the authority of Christ" (I Corinthians 11:5, Phillips' translation).

I am not one to enjoy controversy, to enjoy picking on others, to take pleasure in stirring up trouble, but even "the mild folk" occasionally see red. What has brought fire into my eyes on this subject of pretension within the organized church is an article I read recently. It was written by a popular clergyman of our day.

It was so unintelligible that in order to wade through it I had to lean heavily on a dictionary, a lexicon, and a friend who is steeped in theology. Now if I were reading a paper on jet propulsion or magneto-electric machinery, it would come as no surprise to me that I did not understand it. My mind does not run in those channels. But when a man tells me he is going to state his religious convictions, what he believes concerning the Christian faith, this interests me, and I assume I'll "get" at least every other word, because I, too, have spent some hours these past ten years thinking about the same exciting subject.

I cannot begin to try to interpret for you what he said, but you are not missing anything. His article was dreary, confusing, and ponderous. I had to keep reminding myself this was a supposed confession of the same glorious faith to which I adhere; and yet not once did this theologian affirm any of the great, grand truths that have been lifting men out of darkness into light ever since God revealed Himself to man in this Book of books.

There is a reason why this cleric has nothing hopeful, nothing real, nothing consoling that we, the people, can press to our hearts and say with conviction, "This we can trust," and the reason is tied up in the introduction to his article. It states that this important churchman admitted that he is more liberal in his theology than he was ten years ago. I, too, for awhile thought this was the ideal to be more open-minded about the Bible, but every single person I have known and have read about who has pursued the "liberal" trend has ended up belittling the Bible. And almost worse, they end up spending so much time snipping and chopping away at their Bibles (Don't kid yourself: we all have a broad streak of this love to tear into things, and many a person who has started out with a little pocket knife, soon is slashing away with a saber), they have little time left to enjoy the Word.

Open up the pages of history and see for yourself what has happened to men who have taken God at His Word. There was John Wesley. "The only true and safe religion for Wesley," it was written of him, "be it called one thing or another, is that which is centered on Jesus Christ." The same Book that the higher critics of our day claim "to be full of error and contradiction" caused Wesley to bring thousands into a dynamic, authentic faith, and as a result of one man's complete reliance on Holy Scripture an entire nation was spared a revolution of violence.

Then there was Adolf Hitler who was brought up in a nation where a handful of theologians started pulling apart the Bible, and within a short span of time there was widespread unbelief, although still masquerading under the title of Christianity. I have heard historians cite this as proof that Christianity is dead, because of what happened in that "Christian" nation, Germany. You can pin the label "rose" on an evil-smelling weed, but it will never make it a rose. Over and over since God visited the earth in the person of Jesus Christ, groups of arrogant men have pasted the label "Christianity" on this church and that church, but the true spirit of Christ was no more in the church than the perfume of the rose upon the skunk plant. And so Hitler grew up to hate the Bible because he associated falseness and weakness with the church that was called Christian but was not Christian, and he went on to wreck a continent.

It is not a light thing to treat the Bible as a toy or a tool to be manipulated as man sees fit. As Immanuel Kant said, "The existence of the Bible as a book for the people, is the greatest benefit which the human race has ever experienced. Every attempt to belittle it is a crime against humanity."

It is grand to have a wonderful education, and I have deep respect for persons who believe in developing their minds, but how puny and pathetic to use this gift of God to try to out-think God. There is an area in any dynamic faith where the believer, be he the greatest intellect of his age, quietly says with the common man, "Lord, I believe; help thou my unbelief."

Pascal made this distinction which has helped me see the importance of trusting the Bible, because out of trust comes love:

"Human knowledge must be understood to be loved, but divine knowledge must be loved to be understood."

To go back to the theologian who wrote the article which I could barely understand. Remember, this was his testimony of faith in the same Lord I follow. Surely, shouldn't we, as authentic followers of the Christ, be able to speak of Him as plainly and clearly as He spoke of Himself?

The best way to get a clue what Christianity is about is to listen to the Galilean Himself, "Do you believe me when I say that I am in the Father and the Father in me?" The sincere believer simply nods, "Yes, Lord, I believe." Now the scissor-snipping higher-uppers approach a passage like that this way: "We value the truths that have been passed down through the centuries, but reinterpreted, of course, mythologically. There are several words in this statement that I cannot affirm as literal prose. Take this obscure phrase, 'Do you believe me?' I believe the best way for us to condition our people toward the understanding of obscurantism is through liturgy. Let the people sing these obscure words, a sort of emotion will carry them which will be a positive force. In the final analysis, the best I can answer concerning this passage, I really do not know. These words simply do not speak to me."

I have exaggerated a little, but not much. Higher criticism operates on a logic something like this. We have all heard it said, "An apple a day keeps the doctor away." If that is true, say the belittlers of God's Word, "Two apples a day will keep two doctors away." And the irony of this, those who stand at the opposite pole of mistrust in the Bible, the overtrusters who read more things into it than they ought, do much the same thing. They are the ones who end up with stacks of tired clichés, noisy, unattractive maxims, and seem to buy up all the time on radio, particularly in the South.

I find it even tiresome to talk about this. Let us return to the lovely, hopeful words of the real Christ, "Do you believe me when I say that I am in the Father and the Father in me? . . . I assure you that the man who believes in me will do the same things that I have done, yes, and he will do even greater things than these, for I am going away to the Father. Whatever you ask the Father in my name, I will do — that the Son may bring glory to the Father" (John 14: 10,12 Phillips' translation).

To be sure, you or I won't get anything from those words if we regard them as myth or if we question the authenticity of the author, John, but only if we have a loving trust for our Bibles, as that good man, Abraham Lincoln, had, "I believe the Bible is the best gift God has ever given to man," he wrote. "All the good from the Saviour of the world is communicated to us through this book." If more of us had faith like that, we too might break through to something grand, liberating and uplifting in these awful days of doubt, mistrust and fear.

Learn to love that Book, O learned men, and then stand back and see what God will do with your lives. "In all our ways we are to acknowledge Him, and He will direct our paths." Obscure, confusing words? Yes, to the man who does not believe; but to the one who believes them, they are altogether lovely and brilliant with light.

Perhaps the higher critics of our day need to conduct their meetings on their knees at night under God's sky. As an unknown poet said, "We are such little men when the stars come out."

Spiritual Exercise: As Dwight L. Moody, another grand man of faith, said, "Those who are full of doubts will never be much blessed. The Book comes to us as a whole with the same authority, and no man has a right to cut out any portion." Let us pray that God will give us the eye of faith, so we may learn His deeper truths.

33

EACH TO HIS OWN

Small Talk: There is a trilogy of verses in the Bible which have even deeper significance when the thoughts are joined together: "All we like sheep have gone astray; we have turned every one to his own way, and the Lord hath laid on him the iniquity of us all."

"If we confess our sins, he is faithful and just to forgive us our sins, and to cleanse us from all unrighteousness."

"Now unto him that is able to keep you from falling, and to present you faultless before the presence of his glory with exceeding joy, to the only wise God our Saviour, be glory and majesty, dominion and power, both now and ever. Amen."

All like sheep, all gone astray. I don't find that concept difficult to understand or accept as truth. I have inward eyes and outward eyes. The inward eyes reveal to me clearly that this is a portrait of me, like a sheep, wayward, purposeless, seemingly interested only in grazing, fearful and lost. My outward eyes see much the same picture. Even the greatest of living men and those in history demonstrate such frailty part of the time, a certain something out of kilter which we lamely explain, "He's only human."

What better explanation do you want? We have turned every one to his own way.

In a seemingly simple situation where two people live together, or a family of five, look what chaos can result in days or weeks when each one, or just one of them, turns to his own way. And yet we seem mystified and puzzled at world-wide chaos. Do you want a short answer why the people of this world are still in great travail and confusion? Read the answer in God's Holy Word: "... we have turned every one to his own way." And the weeping and wailing shall go on as long as we, like sheep, insist upon our own way. There is even a shorter answer to chaos, both personal and universal: sin.

There are many "if's" in the Bible, and one of the highest each individual has to hurdle is the one relating to sin. Your sin. My sin. So often we make the mistake of ignoring God's judgment of our waywardness by comparing ourselves with our neighbors. It is quite possible that you are a finer person than the man who lives next door to you, but this waywardness is strictly a matter between God and you. God and me.

If we confess our sins, He is faithful.

And He is so much more, glory and majesty, dominion and power, and more, and more, and more. Merciful and forgiving.

I recently took a bus trip. I hadn't been on a Greyhound bus in years. When I used to ride buses, they were buses. Today we have Scenic-Cruisers equipped with balcony, air-conditioning, cushioned seats and a powder room. Interestingly enough, though, this streamlined beauty had the same old standard human equipment I vividly remember from the past. In the front seat behind the bus driver was an elderly lady with asthma. Directly in back of her and facing the "Smoking in the Rear" sign, were two G. I.'s, both chain smokers, and across the aisle from me a young mother with a baby in arms. The old lady talked and coughed away at the driver, the two young soldiers laughed and smoked, the baby cried, and the Scenic-Cruiser raced up and down the hills of Iowa.

Around three in the morning we stopped in the midst of nowhere and we all yawned our way into the dismal bus depot. We didn't say much as we sat around the counter, but one of the soldiers held the baby while the mother poured sugar into her coffee, and the other fellow passed the cream to the elderly lady before he used it, and the bus driver asked the waitress if her cold was any better. I sat thinking how like life this is — we are truly strangers and pilgrims on this earth and as we jostle along we often annoy one another, but suddenly it doesn't really matter. There is such redemption in small acts of kindness, thoughtfulness, and goodness. Yes, we do turn to our own way much of the time, but happily not all the people all the time.

It was about sunrise as we pulled into Minneapolis, and my mind was dwelling in deep places. I pondered how like life this is, too. At the moment we're closest to understanding what life is about, we have to arouse ourselves and go and live it. How thankful I am that I can live my life in the quiet confidence of hope in the only wise God our Saviour.

Spiritual Exercise: Memorize Isaiah 53:6.

34

UNLIMITED POSSIBILITIES

Small Talk: For Thanksgiving dinner today I had a piece of pea-nut brittle. I am not proving anything, I simply happen to be in that stage of my work when I like to keep going. This, the sparsest of a long line of bountiful Thanksgiving dinners, did underline one thing for me. The only needful morsel to properly celebrate this sacred holiday is a thankful heart. As the church bells outside my hotel window played "Count Your Blessings," I could only whisper the most general, and yet the most personal prayer a per-son can make, "I do thank Thee, O Lord, for everything."

Now back to the book.

You probably would not have picked up this volume if you, too, were not genuinely interested in being more alive. We all, at times, sense an inadequacy in this direction.

I dig my way through some days as if already all but my head were beneath the sod (sometimes all I need is vitamins or a little oxygen, but the answer isn't always that simple). And then, too, I suspect that even after I complete this book, I shall go on having my share of unlively days; but even in acknowledging this, I am moving a step closer to truth, and the more we brush elbows with truth, the more truly we are going to come alive. The truth always means being set free, and when we are free, we're really living.

An author writing in a women's fashion magazine was think-ing along the same line. She said that no matter what you read to the contrary, one thing is certain on our trip through this valley of soul-making. Every so often, we either fall or get pushed. And we have to get up again. We get better at licking our shortcom-ings, but no one ever got them licked once and for all. There are popular psychiatrists and clergymen who will tell you it isn't so, but St. Paul knew better, and so should you if the next bump isn't going to leave you flatter than the last.

One of the more maddening aspects of middle age is that you are middle-aged. You get up in the morning and while brushing your teeth you catch a glimpse of yourself in the mirror. You really wish you could skip the whole thing, go back to bed, and not impose yourself on the world. If only it were permissible in our culture to look middle-aged. But oh no! You must look young. You have to look young. You would practically die on the spot if the first person you met on the way to the office exclaimed, "My, you look pleasant and middle-aged today!"

I keep asking myself, what is so wrong about being middle-aged? I am speaking more specifically about the years between forty and fifty, the years middle age closes in on you. You can't walk away from it. It moves right in. In fact, it fastens on to you, generally around the waist and hips, that is unless you out-run it or out-steam it.

Then it grabs hold of the mind and causes you to whine, "Shut that door, John, I can feel a draft way in here," or "Go into business with you? Not me, I'm 49 and I'm not taking any risks," or "Walk with you to the grocery store? Are you out of your mind? That's five blocks away!" This go-away-and-let-me-rest mentality also needs ventilating, steaming and out-running.

And as if we haven't woes enough as we slide into the middle-age groove, we start getting anxious about all that we haven't done. We begin to persecute ourselves as we examine the difference between what we have achieved and what we feel we ought to have achieved. It can become such a concern that the very worry about how little we have done and how late it is can drain the energy we do have and actually make us tired and old long before our rendezvous with old age.

What is the answer for us poor, old middle-aged people? Is there an answer? Will I have this heavy, anxious feeling the rest of my days? Is there anything to look forward to now that I am no longer chronologically young?

In answer, let me share with you a story I heard last week. When George Bernard Shaw was ninety, he heard a friend of his bemoaning the fact that it was his fiftieth birthday.

Shaw looked at the man and said, "You should be happy instead of downcast, you foolish fellow! You have escaped the forties, which are the old age of youth and are embarking on the fifties, which are the glorious youth of old age!"

That is answer enough for me. I can bump my way through anything as long as I know it gets better ahead.

In the final analysis I think the secret to large living is in the recognition that every day is a new day, and within the limitations of that one day, you and I have unlimited possibilities for making it a glorious day, and I don't really think it makes too much difference where we stand on the ladder, in the middle, at the bottom rung or at the top, chronologically, materially or intellectually.

Living is and has always been a moment-by-moment affair, and all the foolishness about saying we're too old to do this or too young or too middle-aged is a device of Satan to keep us from daring great things for God.

Spiritual Exercise: As we begin tomorrow, we will undoubtedly think of ten or twelve things that need our immediate attention. Let us go and do one of them.

35

MOSES LISTENS

Small Talk: It is common to make jokes about in-laws, particularly mothers-in-law. It is sad but true that there have been and are enough "good" examples of bad in-laws in every community around the globe to give credence to the stories. Thus it is refreshing to hear a story about a good in-law, this time a father-in-law. His name is Jethro.

Jethro could have been suspicious of his son-in-law, Moses, because the young man appears on the scene rather mysteriously. This is generally fertile field for the in-law trouble, but Jethro apparently trusted Moses from their first meeting.

All goes well for a number of years, and then one day when

Moses was attending his father-in-law's flock, he had an extra-ordinary experience. This could have been the end of their good relationship. Moses was only a shepherd, whereas Jethro was a priest. And so when Moses came and told his father-in-law that God had spoken to him and he must go back to Egypt, a lesser man would not have been able to take it. *Why should God speak to this peasant, my daughter's husband. After all, I, Jethro, am the servant of God; and furthermore, I'm not going to support his wife and children while he runs off. A good son-in-law stays home and looks after his family.* But no, Jethro did not think this way. These were his words to Moses, "Go in peace."

Many years went by, and Moses had to send back his wife and children to his father-in-law. Those must have been anxious years. Probably they never really knew if they would see Moses again.

Then next we have this lovely scene portrayed for us in the eighteenth chapter of Exodus: "When Jethro, the priest of Midian, Moses' father-in-law, heard of all that God had done for Moses, and for Israel his people, and that the Lord had brought Israel out of Egypt; then Jethro . . . came with his sons and his wife unto Moses into the wilderness, where he encamped at the mount of God."

By this time in the story Moses is already a great man. He is the chosen leader of a great company of people, his responsi-bilities are tremendous, and it would have been easy for Jethro to fall into the pit of idolizing his now famous son-in-law. But their relationship did not change. "Moses went out to meet his father-in-law, and did obeisance, and kissed him; and they asked each other of their welfare; and they came into the tent."

There is considerable tenderness in the remark, "They asked each other of their welfare." Moses was as interested in the folks back home as they were in him. Probably they shed some tears together, and then after the "small talk," Moses shared with his father-in-law all that the Lord had done in the fantastic deliverance from Egypt, and Jethro rejoiced.

Moses cordially told his father-in-law to "make himself at home," and so the next day Jethro wandered about the camp getting acquainted. He was particularly interested in one of Moses' many responsibilities.

"What is this thing you're doing for the people?" he asked. "Why are you sitting out here alone, and all the people lining up from morning until evening?"

Moses explained that the people came to him to inquire about God, and that he also served as their judge. Jethro did not say anything right away. He continued observing until he had all the facts.

Later that night in the tent he said, "Moses, listen to me. You're going to wear yourself out if you keep up this pace. Do you think you will be any benefit to God or to these people if you have a nervous breakdown?"

Moses sighed deeply from the couch, "I know, I know, Father. It distresses me greatly, but the people clamor about me, and I feel I must help them."

Jethro looked directly into the eyes of his son-in-law and said gently, "Moses, my son, you are not the first nor the last of God's chosen ones who fail to recognize there are others in God's kingdom equally as able as you to minister to the needs of the people."

Jethro said no more, but continued to gaze deep into Moses. Moses shifted uncomfortably and lowered his eyes. Finally he said quietly, "Jethro, I'm afraid you are penetrating into my inner heart." He paused, then said slowly, "I'm afraid you're right. I have been thinking I am the only one."

He wearily pulled himself to a standing position. He walked over and put his arm around his father-in-law.

"What do you suggest I do?"

Here we see the real stature of Moses. There is a proverb that goes, "It does not matter whether good counsel comes from small or great — to those who profit by it."

Jethro had a genius for organization. He had Moses choose able men and make them rulers over thousands, hundreds, fifties, and tens. He taught him how to use others to bear the burden with him. He showed him how to save his strength and gifts for the tasks that only he could do.

When Jethro was satisfied that things were going well with

his son-in-law, he announced his departure. "It is time for me to depart into my own land," he said. Moses and the people urged him to stay with them, but here we see the stature of Jethro. The wise-in-law knows when it is best to leave.

Spiritual Lesson: Read Exodus, chapters 2, 3 and 4 and chapter 18.

36

SIGH AND MOAN ALONE

Small Talk: "I've noticed something, Mother," the young daughter of a friend of mine said the other noon when these two were doing dishes together. "I've noticed that not many people are cheery like you."

That is a lovely tribute paid to a mother, and from one of the toughest critics, her own daughter who sees her pretty much as she is. What a fine and noble thing it is to be a pleasant person, and above all, to be pleasant so your immediate family is aware of it!

We're all fairly adept at painting a smile on our faces when we meet a new person, walk into the bank, or stand up to make an announcement at a meeting. In fact, some of us are positively *charming* on these occasions. Yet how tragic and true to life to find out that some of these charmers are the world's worst battle-axes in the privacy of their own circle of friends and relatives, where they are just being themselves.

They are the ones who are always on the phone, "Did I blow my top this morning. I really told my husband and the children and his mother where to get off! I've just had enough of their ordering *me* around. Say, did you happen to see that ridiculous hat Elizabeth was wearing...oh, you know, Elizabeth, my husband's sister..."

To be cheerful and nice to the people with whom we live

and do with day in and day out — this takes maturity. This requires Christian love, the real thing, not a home-frabricated sort with directions from a "do-it-yourself" kit. This genuine love comes from within where the Spirit of God has changed the natural heart which is selfish, proud, cruel, and a lot of other strong-smelling adjectives which most of us dislike associating with ourselves.

Cheeriness cannot be faked.

I am continually awed at the high cost of a beautiful smile. In the case of my cheery friend, on the surface she would seem to have everything, as if it were natural and spontaneous for her to be happy. She is attractive and has a warm personality. Her interests are varied and wide, and whatever she does, she does whole-heartedly and with an enthusiasm that is catching. Also she has a lovely family, fine husband, no financial worries — why shouldn't she be cheery?

Ah yes, but that is the surface picture. We are awfully quick to assume that those who don't wear their agonies stamped on their faces nor pouring out of their mouths in long tales of woe, have none. In truth, few lives escape pain, and there is a form of heart and mind agony that is so acute and imperious that it makes all other suffering seem light-hearted in comparison. Don't be too sure that the next "happy" person you meet isn't well acquainted with grief and a silent man of sorrows.

I do know that my good friend has a few complicated, heart-rending frustrations in her life that could easily cast a veil of gloom over her and all those she loves if she let them overcome her. But she has turned over these twisted, heavy weights that are straining to pull the smile from her lovely face to the Christ whose peace is stronger than man's agony. And onward she goes, being cheerful for the sake of others; and then she has the promise that all things are to be judged righteously, maybe not tomorrow, but someday, and so why not sing a little in anticipation?

The small daughter's observation was piercing. There are not many people who are cheery. And in most situations the fault is ours, as much as we love to point our fingers here, there, and everywhere. I do not know who wrote it, but a portion of a poem comes to mind.

> "If you have to sigh or moan,
> Do it while you are alone."

And I would add, *alone with God*. Our amazing God who through His Son has told us, "Why are ye fearful, O ye of little faith? Be of good cheer; I have overcome the world."

Spiritual Exercise: Gertrude Stein said something I have never forgotten, "Everyone when they are young has a little bit of genius — that is, they really do listen. They can listen and talk at the same time. Then they grow older and many of them get tired and they listen less and less. But some, a very few, continue to listen."

Make a particular point of listening tomorrow. Observe the people with whom you work and live, not clinically and crudely, but quietly and kindly. Be on the lookout for the cheery people. Particularly listen to them.

Small Prayer: Lord, help me to honestly face the sort of a person I am, and if I am not one of the pleasant ones, help me to become one. Amen. Read Romans chapter 8.

Conclusion:

Lovingly

*And now abideth faith, hope, love, these three; but the
greatest of these is love.* I Corinthians 13:13

37

LOVE AND FORGIVE

Small Talk: When the bus came, I followed a neighbor in and
she invited me to sit with her. I was fairly new to the neighborhood, but you soon get to recognize faces. At the next corner,
another neighbor got on. She and I exchanged greetings. I
noticed that she only spoke to me. When she moved to the rear
of the bus, I said to the lady sitting next to me, "Is that who I
thought it was, Mrs. Allen, who lives next door to you?"

The woman replied coldly, "She lives there, all right, but
I'd just as soon she lived on the other side of the moon."

I later learned that my two neighbors had at one time been
fast friends, but a misunderstanding which they never took pains
to unravel had blown up into this pitiless silence. This is trag-
edy. There is enough in life to lose heart about without adding
this heart-hardener to our already burdened lives. I take it very,
very seriously when friends become strangers, nay, worse than
that, enemies, because I am beginning to see something tremendous about the love of God. Until recently I saw the love of
God as something between God and me, with Christ, of course,
as the Mediator. It is most certainly unthinkable to talk about
the love of God and leave out the Saviour. But by the same
token there is nothing to the love of God which leaves out others. God continually shows His love to us in and through others.
We're all in this thing together. Dostoevsky expresses in his novels the thought that every crime is not only a sin of the criminal,
but also a sin of the community and of society; no one has a
right to say that he has no share in the guilt of the guilty. Then

in *Crime and Punishment* Dostoevsky develops the idea that all humanity is — one man. I would say yes, in the sense that Christ died for all. "For the love of Christ constraineth us; because we thus judge, that if one died for all, then were all dead: And that he died for all, that they which live should not henceforth live unto themselves, but unto him which died for them, and rose again." But we come to Christ one by one, and we henceforth no longer live unto ourselves.

This tells me in no uncertain terms that the love of God has everything in the world to do with people, (brothers and sisters who no longer speak, friends who are politely cool with one another, fathers who have disowned sons) forgiving and loving one another. Loving and forgiving. It is in the measure in which we love and forgive, and are loved and forgiven, that we experience the real, deep-down love of God.

I am finally convinced that one of the paramount reasons we are receiving so little of God's love today is not because God has little love to give, but because we have little room in our hearts for His love. Our hearts are crowded and choked with envying, jealousy, self-adoration, pet theories, selfish whims and unforgiveness. It takes too much out of us to really love people.

We prefer to gather together in groups, repeat words, say a few prayers, sing a song, pledge a dollar or two, work for a good cause, write books, show our interest in the heathen abroad; *anything* but walk across the room or a few blocks up the street and throw our arms around someone who desperately needs our love and forgiveness. It costs a lot to forgive, but there is no reward to equal it. All benefit from forgiveness. When I remember Christ's words to His tormentors, then I know I can forgive any man anything. "Father, forgive them," said this One who died for all, "for they know not what they do."

They know not what they do, but He has taught us what to do. Love and forgive.

Spiritual Exercise: Read Luke 23:20-49.

38

SHE SHARED HER SAVIOUR

Small Talk: "Mother, you can sit in this comfortable chair and ...." The upright, seventy-year-old woman looked at her daughter and said, "Posh."

"You know perfectly well, Addie," the older lady continued, "I've never sat in comfortable chairs, and I'm not changing my ways simply because I've come to live with you. No, I shall have to be busy, and I'm sure the Lord will give me something to do."

And He did. By four that afternoon Mrs. VanCamp had circled the neighborhood. "You might as well come right out and tell me, Mother," Addie said as she helped her mother out of her coat. "I know you're up to something."

Mrs. VanCamp bent over to take off her boots. It was a raw winter day in Minneapolis and she had walked several blocks. She said in an offhand way, "I've invited a few of our neighbors in for coffee Thursday morning."

"That's tomorrow," Addie exclaimed. "What in the world are you thinking of? We have to feed them, clean the house, the basement is a mess. Why, I don't know any of these women — oh, Mother!"

"I don't either. That's why I thought it would be nice if we all got acquainted," and with a look of mischief in her brown eyes, "I won't let one of them down in the basement!"

Addie didn't have the courage to ask how many were coming, but when she saw her mother get out the largest mixing bowl, she knew it was more than a few.

The two ladies worked until late that night, and her mother's happy bustling about in the kitchen caused a couple of tears to fall on the silverware Addie was polishing, but then she too caught the fun and found herself humming a cheerful tune as she put the living room in order.

The "few" ladies (as Addie told a friend later, "I honestly believe there were over thirty") whirled into the living room around ten the next morning. It was snowing outside, and it put everyone in high spirits as they stamped their feet and shook the soft flakes from their coats. "Don't you love walking in the snow?" Mrs. VanCamp said to the group that had just blown into the room. "To tell the truth, Mrs. VanCamp," one large, smartly-dressed lady replied, "that's the first winter walk I've had in twenty years." A suggestion of a grin played around her mouth, "Yes, you're right, it was rather nice."

Addie's mother was a marvel as a hostess. She was gliding around the room making sure that Mrs. Smith knew Mrs. Stockland who lived down the street and around the corner, and that Mrs. Tessler had met the pretty little Chinese lady who lived above the meat market.

After everyone had plenty of time to talk and laugh and taste the homemade coffee cake and butter cookies and enjoy good, hot cups of coffee, Mrs. VanCamp struck a chord on the piano to get the attention of all.

"You all seem to be having a good time," she said sincerely. "I can't tell you how happy I am to move into a neighborhood with so many lovely people."

She smiled around the room. "I'm in favor of our getting together like this once a week."

There was a quick response of enthusiasm.

"Fine," continued Mrs. VanCamp. "Now it impresses me that if we just get together every week and only talk, we're apt to end up talking about the neighbors who aren't here, so maybe we better plan to do something. We could sew perhaps or read some of Ibsen's plays, or I suppose we could study the prophets of the Old Testament — well, you suggest to me what you want to do."

It was young Mrs. Hagadorn who had moved into the neighborhood just a few days before Mrs. VanCamp who said, "It would mean something to me to study the Bible. We don't have an adult class in our church any longer, and I miss it."

"All right then," Mrs. VanCamp replied. "We'll study the

Bible. You all come back next Thursday at ten, and we'll have another good time together."

And the neighbors kept coming and coming and Mrs. Van-Camp never did sit in the comfortable chair. And when they buried her in her 82nd year, the neighbors came again to her daughter's home. "And the things they told me," Addie said softly, "are almost too wonderful to repeat. I guess Mrs. Wong who lives above the meat market said it the best, 'I shall be always loving your mother more than anyone in America, because she not only shared herself but her Saviour with me, one of her neighbors.'"

Spiritual Exercise: Ask God to show you if there is some small way you can extend His love to one of your neighbors. Read Matthew 12:46-50; Matthew 20:28; John 9:4,5; Galatians 6:1-10; Isaiah 58:10-14.

39

WHAT POWER IN LOVE

Small Talk: A friend whom I have known since childhood wrote to me recently. She had read the article in which I had jokingly commented that the trouble with middle age is that you're middle-aged. "Don't be depressed," she said. "Just think, we have survived viruses and vehicles, homework, practicing, shyness, pimples and giggles, depressions, wars, parties and proms, hate, grief. As we are learning more about God, we are beginning to realize we aren't ever going to be perfect in this life, but we can live with this limitation if we acquaint ourselves with the most beautiful word in the English language, love."

She finished her note to me, "What power we have when we can love!"

My friend and I seldom see each other now, because we no longer live in the same town; but, in very truth, nothing, no nothing, can untie our friendship now and forever, as long as we continue to make love our great quest.

Ever so often I read Dostoevsky, as you have already gathered. I read a lot of other books, but I keep going back to the Russian, because he, too, believed there is power in love and threaded this theme in and out of his novels. You have to work to find the gold in Dostoevsky's writings, because he is as long-winded as a blizzard that sweeps uninterrupted across the Russian steppes, and often as chilling and depressing, but buried in the drifts of words are unforgettable scenes.

Like this one in *Letters from the Underworld*. The central character of the book, a cynical debauchee, is speaking to a woman of the streets, who is obviously a newcomer to this "profession."

"Yesterday," he said, "I saw some men carrying a coffin. They very nearly let it fall."

Then in vivid language he pictures to her what will be her end if she goes on in this sordid business. He doesn't judge (he is hardly in the position, being an outcast of society himself); he simply presents facts.

After awhile she says icily, "Ah, well — then I must die, that is all."

"But do you not at all regret it?"

"Regret what?"

"Your life."

There came no answer.

The man continued,

"Have you ever had a sweetheart?"

She answered,

"What is that to you?"

These are the same words Jesus used to still Peter when that impetuous one was asking more than he ought. "What is that to you, Peter?" said the Christ. "You follow me."

I do not believe that it is a coincidence that Dostoevsky put those words in the mouth of the prostitute, "What is that to you?" because in the next few pages follows one of the Russian novelist's hauntingly beautiful love passages. He has the embittered, lonely, unloved man of the underworld pour out to Lisa what his life could have been had he ever known love, and what her life could still be if she will open her heart to love. Real love.

For Dostoevsky, a sick, lonely, brilliant, and unstable man himself, love is the panacea for the sicknesses and sins of humanity, love, yes, love, and again love — love in the highest and most noble sense of the word. Love that is fragrant with forgiveness, kind, gentle, pure and good, not irritable, not conceited, not jealous, not touchy, but decent, straight, undying, love which believes the best of every person, and hopes under all circumstances and can outlast anything. Love, which most of his characters hardly ever experienced even a glimmer, but this compassionate Russian saw that even in the most degraded of human beings, in the foulest of surroundings, there is always the possibility of a shaft of light rending the blackness and love breaking through to redeem the lost.

Yes, I read Dostoevsky. Not for amusement — he seldom entertains. Many of his word pictures of life are appalling, and perhaps for some, too appalling; but they do what they are supposed to. They leave the reader with the uneasy sensation that he hasn't begun to grasp the depth and height and width of love, God's love.

Spiritual Exercise: "For God so loved the world . . . ." What do those words mean? "Dear Lord, teach me about love." Read I John 3:11-18.

40

ONLY LENT

Small Talk: I came on this poem the other day, and it had run in an Indianapolis paper on the day of James Whitcomb Riley's death in 1916:

> *Well, good-by, Jim; take keer yerself!*
> *Yer dead, but still you'll live*
> *In human hearts as long as God*
> *Has human life to give.*

> *You b'longed to Him, Jim, anyway,*
> *An' you was only lent:*
> *A nation's everlastin' love*
> *Shall be yer monument.*
> —*Bide Dudley*

Recently I have been having a good time re-reading some of the poets I studied in school. It is easy in the process of getting educated to miss the entire point. I was reminded of this yesterday while talking with a freshman home from college. She was telling me about a term paper she had just handed in on Shakespeare,

"Glad I don't have to think about him again as long as I live."

When I was her age I said much the same thing, and it has taken me years to learn that I had thrown the baby out with the bath water. Until I started reading Shakespeare, Milton, Robert Browning, William Blake, Tennyson, and yes, James Whitcomb Riley, for myself, without the pressure of examinations and term papers, I had no idea how important these poets and many, many others were to become in my life.

Poetry, music, and art are to the human soul what wings are to an eagle. They lift the spirit of man above earth's meanness and travail into the blue sky and on toward the sunrise. They remind the quick-to-forget heart of man that even one daffodil on a mountainside, a border of blue bonnets around an oil field in Texas, a blanket of sun-flowers on the plains of Kansas, one dandelion brashly standing in a velvet green lawn in Oak Park are truly as miraculous as Paul's conversion on the road to Damascus, or my finding peace with God in the Swiss Alps, or your turning to Christ this very day.

I liked that line in the poem about James Whitcomb Riley, "You b'longed to Him, Jim, anyway, An' you was only lent." That by itself would have caused me to bend my way against the snow and wind of Minnesota to the library where I could learn more about this poet. These "lent" ones of God interest me, and I continue to find them in surprisingly different places.

Many I meet in the pages of books. Then once in awhile I meet one of God's "lent" people in an old folks' home. I met two Saturday.

We were seated close to the chair of the dainty, old lady because her hearing and sight were nearly gone. She was telling my friend and me how kind everyone was to her at the home, especially Martin, one of the orderlies.

"He should have been a doctor," she said. Her voice was unusually warm and rich. "When he lifts me back into bed, I always know it is Martin, even though I can't see him, by the way I float down. Some of the nurses and doctors drop you like a lump of clay. O, they don't mean to be rough, they just don't think."

When a bent, elderly man moved softly into the room to empty the waste basket, we knew it was Martin, Martin who belongs to Him and is only lent, lent for a service of love in a place so many people dread going to.

But we need not dread any place if we belong to Him. Our Lord has a way of making every place and any place home when we take Him with us in our hearts.

Another one of God's "lent" ones, expressed it this way:

> *He that has light with his own clear breast*
> *May sit i' the center, and enjoy bright day;*
> *But he that hides a dark soul and foul thoughts*
> *Benighted walks under the midday sun;*
> *Himself in his own dungeon.*
>
> *— John Milton*

Spiritual Exercise: If you do not own any poetry books, walk to the library and see what you can find. A good starting point is with some of those you "hated" in school. You're probably like my college friend and me — you don't dislike the poets, it was the way they were presented.

Lift up your hearts and feast on the writings of two of God's great poets: David and Solomon.

Read Psalms 42 and 43 and Song of Solomon.

41

YOU DON'T UNDERSTAND

Small Talk: A mother and father were having rough days and sleepless nights with their son. The young man was forever in trouble. One day a friend of the father said, "Thomas, if Bill were my boy, I'd let him go."

The friend meant it well. He was distressed to see what this irresponsible, lust-propelled boy was doing to his best friend. The father answered in this manner, "Yes, Jim, if Bill were your boy I'd let him go, too, but you see, he's my boy."

That story has a familiar ring, because it is being enacted all over the world wherever there are caring parents and wayward sons and daughters. Recently I was in the home of a family who had just brought their only son to the State Hospital for the third time. His was a common crippler (at least, when you read statistics it is common today), alcoholism. But there is nothing common about it when you look away from the crying mother and the bewildered father and hear him murmur, "That's my son in there, you don't understand, he's my boy!"

It is so easy for those of us on the sidelines to offer advice and make long speeches to the parents of sons and daughters who have gone astray, but I believe this father is declaring a solemn truth when he says, "You don't understand."

The man of little sensitivity has an explanation and theory for every problem in life. Shakespeare once said, "Every one can master a grief but he that hath it." I, for one, am beginning to develop a great respect for mystery. I have no quick panaceas to hand to those enfolded in tragic situations.

A few years ago I saw a picture in the newspaper of a woman being sent to prison for armed robbery. All I could think as I looked at that sad face, this woman needs a friend. So I wrote to her. After I mailed the letter, I felt foolish. She'll think

I'm a religious crackpot or worse, that I have some "angle." But as it turned out, she did need a friend, and some of her letters during these past five years have been the most rewarding I have ever received.

In yesterday's note she said, "Not too long ago a tour came through the institution, and I heard one of the women say, 'How in the world do people get into such jams?' During the day I thought to myself, *evidently that woman hasn't gone far in understanding."*

Quite a few of us haven't gone far in understanding. No, we don't understand. Here is still another man who didn't understand. He is a Bible teacher and he was commenting on King David's attitude after he had been told that his son Absalom had been killed.

If you recall the story, Absalom was one of the wayward sons of David. To put it mildly, he was a troublemaker, always in difficulties, and finally he decides he would make a better king than his old father.

In the conspiracy against David, Absalom is killed. When David is brought the news, he cries, "O my son Absalom, my son, my son Absalom! would God I had died for thee, O Absalom, my son, my son!"

Here is the Bible teacher's comment on the passage: "David's care for Absalom was not fair to the army which went out to protect him and his realm; nor was it fair to the victorious loyalists, who that day restored him to the throne, to drown the joy of success in grief for the worthless son."

No, many of us haven't gone far in understanding, including a few Bible teachers. True, David's grief probably wasn't fair to the army which had gone out to fight for him, but I do not believe that is the point.

The point is that Absalom was David's son, and David loved his son, yes, his worthless son. Frankly, I love David all the more for mourning Absalom on that day of victory. Give us more men like David who know there is more to life than winning back thrones.

When God's love is embedded in our hearts, we can never cease caring for those we love, even those who let us down. We love them to the end, whether they return the love or not. There is a Latin proverb, "Loyalty is the holiest good in the human heart." The longer I think upon that, the more convinced I am it is true.

The greatest love that any of us will ever experience is the love of God in Christ for us. Here is the same picture we have been talking about, a wayward son or daughter and a father's unending love. I believe that one of the reasons David was able to go on despite his overwhelming losses and personal tragedies was his insight into the peace-bringing truth that God never really lets go of His children, no matter what.

It was David who wrote, "From the end of the earth will I cry unto thee, when my heart is overwhelmed: lead me to the rock that is higher than I." And David's loving Heavenly Father never did let him down when David, in brokenness and contrition, cried for mercy. God always lovingly lifted him up.

Spiritual Exercise: Is there anyone you have let down? Pray afresh that you might be a loyal wife, a loyal friend, a loyal husband to the end. Read Psalm 61.

42

ON THE RIGHT TRACK

"People don't need our criticism, they need our love," said Eugenia Price to an audience in Minneapolis a few years ago, and I have never forgotten that remark.

The thought has been hanging on a wall in my mind, for lo, these many months, much the way people hang framed mottos on the walls in living rooms, "Home is where your heart is," or like that of my friend, Marj, who recently moved into a small trailer, "Home was never like this!"

Don't you sometimes marvel at our collective perspicacity (I'm speaking about the entire human race) to detect the great failings of others and our overwhelming blindness to our own shortcomings? Generous people overlook faults and fix their attention on whatever might be good in the other fellow. People bent on showing their knowledge, superiority, skill and fine backgrounds by constantly picking on others, also reveal something else, their smallness.

There are solemn moments in life, though, when the only loving thing to do is to criticize. Our gentle Lord did not always have a gentle tongue in all situations, but that is the point. He used judgment and only criticized when nothing else would get through to the person. And here is where we fail so often — we criticize too soon and too much.

But criticize we must sometimes, and it is a hard thing to do no matter which side of the fence you are on, but I can honestly say I am thankful that on a couple of occasions a friend has challenged me to think through my actions; to ponder what I believe, to cause me to admit, "You're probably right."

Frankly, how else do we grow? But we do not need to overdo criticizing, nor be harsh and unfair in our distribution of it.

The world is sufficiently noisy from the tearing of men's reputations and characters. Why should I add to it? No, I need to forcefully remind myself every day that people have a far greater need for love, than for criticism, a love I can give to them only because I have experienced the mystical yet very real love of God, perhaps best expressed in the words of Christ, "Father, forgive them: for they know not what they do."

Also I find I am less inclined to criticize as I grow older, because I have by now had enough of a taste of life to know how hard it is to move in a consistently upward pattern. I keep thinking maybe other people find it hard to steer a straight course, too; maybe they have heartaches I know nothing about; maybe they've tried to say something and the wrong words came out.

There was another person who heard Eugenia Price speak that night in Minnesota, a young and brilliant writer who had received nothing but criticism in her three brief months of being a Christian. Everyone was trying to reform her all at once. "I was ready to chuck the whole thing and go back to my old life," she told me one night when I had stopped out at the trailer for a cup of coffee and stayed until two in the morning, "but after I heard that message about love, I knew I was on the right track."

Marj is far from what you would call "a conventional Christian," but she is ideally fitted for the job God had in mind for her. She is sort of "the village priest" in a rundown trailer camp. One small clue that Christ is making an entrance into this loose living community, there is no swearing in front of Marj, be it man, woman or child, and on more than one occasion a little fellow has burst open Marj's door with a bloody nose or a black eye and apologized to her because he forgot he doesn't swear anymore and his friends had reminded him that he *doesn't*.

Spiritual Exercise: "There are diversities of operations, but it is the same God which worketh all in all" I Corinthians 12:6. I notice that I am inclined to criticize people when they do things quite differently than I do, but "there are diversities of operations." It took my friend Marj and me a long time "to accept one another." We had such differences, but the thing that set us free to enjoy one another and to learn from one another, was this simple yet rarely considered truth: People are different. And may I add: let them be different, and from the time you do, you'll be astonished how many nice, really nice people there are in the world, Different! but nice. Prayerfully consider I Corinthians chapter 12 and 13.

43

NO END

Last night as I was swept along in the mob doing last minute shopping in Chicago's Loop, above the noise and confusion could be heard church bells ringing out the immortal hymn, "Joy to the world, the Lord is come!"

That passage from the Christmas story was just fresh in my ears, "And of His kingdom there shall be no end." No end, no end! No wonder that music soars above all this earthly confusion. Joy to the world.

The statement might sound puffed up, "And of His kingdom there shall be no end," because it is of such magnitude and sweep that it barely sounds true, but it comes from the most authoritative and exalted Book on earth, and the words are spoken by an angel, an angel sent from God to tell Mary and all the rest of us who have ears to hear, "And of His kingdom there shall be no end."

These words fall a little hard on our ears in these days. It would seem that this kingdom spoken about two thousand years ago has hardly begun. But even an airy and vague mind like mine can discern that if something shall never end, it must mean that it has begun.

I finally made my way through the crowd to Congress Street and Michigan Blvd., my goal for the evening. One of the drugstore gang had told me I must see the "big tree."

As I stood looking up at the largest and most splendidly decorated Christmas tree I have ever seen (the candy canes alone seemed a story high), I tried to imagine how Christ would react if He were here to celebrate His birthday with us.

I think He would say first, "All this for Me?" But because He is kind, He would add, "How nice." He knows only too well our garish, bragging ways, but would pretend not to be offended by the glitter. And then I think He would look at each one of us, much the way He looked at Peter, when Peter, "the rock," denied Him. "There is only one thing lacking." His words would be gentle but devastating, "You have forgotten to give Me your hearts."

And even as we would stand there in the cold, our hearts would be strangely warm as the people would swarm about Him bringing their children to Him, and He would take them in His arms and put His hands upon them and bless them, and it would be the happiest, gentlest Christmas ever, and all the people would sing, "Joy to the world, the Lord is come!"

And one tiny child would say in a loud voice, "Mamma, I like this man better than Santa Claus."

Spiritual Exercise: Let us start preparing for next Christmas now by giving Him back the gift of ourselves. Read the book of John.

44

HE IS PRECIOUS

Small Talk: Anton Chekhov begins one of his short stories: "The town was small— no better than a village — and it was inhabited almost entirely by old people who died so seldom that it was positively painful."

With only that evidence you would think Chekhov had something against old people, but that was not the case. He was establishing a mood. The story is about a coffin maker, and from the point of view of a coffin maker, this is not a good situation when people refuse to die. "In one word," Chekhov commented, "business was bad."

Nearly every attitude we have in life is colored by the point of view we take. There was John Newton, a wreck of a man if ever there was one. Had he visited Chicago in this century, he would have found his way to "Skid Row" within an hour after he left his ship. He was a hard, rough, dirty sailor with a foul mouth and an appetite for rotten living.

He hated life and life hated him.

Someone placed in the hands of this derelict a copy of Thomas á Kempis' *The Imitation of Christ*. Then a fearful experience in a storm at sea, together with his recovery from a dreaded illness in Africa, brought Newton to the point of view where he began to wonder about God. He had had the gift of a good mother, and she had taught him what she knew about the Scriptures, but she had died when he was seven, and with his father at sea, from that time on he had been left to shift largely for himself.

John Newton struggled to find peace with God for six years after his illness and his first brush with the Eternal One. He made a sincere attempt to live a life of integrity and his battles with himself were fierce. On his last voyage out as the captain of a slaveship, he had the good fortune to meet a man who helped bring him to faith in Christ.

From then on, the point of view of John Newton changed. He began to love life and life loved him. He gave people the impression that he knew a marvelous secret. And he went all about England sharing the secret.

When he was well past the "retirement age," he had to have an assistant stand in the pulpit with him on Sundays to help him read his sermons. He was nearly blind, but nothing could keep this man from preaching while he still had breath.

One Sunday while delivering his message he repeated the sentence, "Jesus Christ is precious."

His helper whispered nervously,

"You've already said that twice."

Newton turned in the direction of his friend and said loudly, "Yes, I've said it twice, and I'm going to say it again."

The stones in the ancient sanctuary fairly shook as the grand old preacher said again, "Jesus Christ is precious!"

I would have loved to have been there that day to experience the joyfulness of that moment. When isn't it glorious to hear a man speak lovingly about His Lord?

Jesus Christ was precious to John Newton.

Many of us today remember him only as the author of several notable hymns and as a friend and associate of the Wesley brothers, Whitefield, and William Cowper. But John Newton never forgot who he was: a former libertine, a former slave captain, a former lost and lonely and unloved seaman. No wonder his words quicken the hearts of all of us who also have learned that Jesus Christ is precious.

Spiritual Exercise: Depending on your mood, play any of the following recordings: Bach's *St. Matthews Passion,* Verdi's *Requiem Mass,* selections from Handel's *Messiah,* Mozart's

Requiem, or any majestic choral music. But perhaps you feel like me and want only to sit quietly and hum John Newton's hymn, "Amazing Grace."

Finish this small study by reading that marvelous hymn of praise, Psalm 107.

> *Now our Lord Jesus Christ Himself, and God, even our Father, which hath loved us, and hath given us everlasting consolation and good hope through grace.*
>
> *Comfort your hearts and mine, and stablish us in every good word and work; and to Thee, precious Lord, we give all honor and glory. Amen.*